SLOW FINANCE

Slow Finance

Why Investment Miles Matter

GERVAIS WILLIAMS

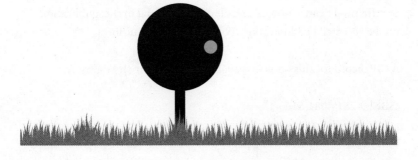

BLOOMSBURY

First published in the United Kingdom in 2011 by

Bloomsbury Publishing Plc
50 Bedford Square
London
WC1B 3DP

A CIP record for this book is available from the British Library.

ISBN: 9-781-4081-5163-1

This book is produced using paper that is made from wood grown in managed, sustainable forests. It is natural, renewable and recyclable. The logging and manufacturing processes conform to the environmental regulations of the country of origin.

Design by Fiona Pike, Pike Design, Winchester
Typeset by Saxon Graphics Ltd, Derby
Printed in the United Kingdom by Martins The Printers,
Berwick-upon-Tweed

In memorium
Nicholl Williams

Contents

List of illustrations

Acknowledgements

Writing a book has always felt like attempting to scale the Matterhorn to me; a nice thought from the hotel balcony but something of a nightmare on an icy ledge halfway up. But after I left Gartmore, I realised that if I was ever to achieve it, now was the time.

I don't regard myself as a natural writer, so this task has taken me outside my comfort zone. To attempt it, I knew I would have to rely heavily on a team who would help me along the way, and I have been extraordinarily fortunate to find one that has offered unreserved support. BJ Cunningham deserves immense credit for his enthusiasm, and for passing on his tips regarding getting the book off in its first teetering steps.

Susan Lawson came in, right from the start, with pertinent and accurate comments about the whole process of writing a book. She patiently dealt with my inexperience, helping me pull together my ideas into a structure that had a proper logical order. Though she does not have a financial background, she seemed at ease with the subject matter and asked well-targeted and pertinent questions, and provided some ideas on where to look for the answers. Some of her questions helped me to articulate ideas that were still unformed in my mind at the start of the process. Susan has had a tremendously valuable role in helping make this book relevant.

Mark Johnstone has given immense support in taking the early ideas and helping to flesh them out. He put a huge amount of time into researching some of the concepts, finding new texts, articulating different ways of getting ideas on the page, listing different attributes and critiquing some of my early script. Mark, along with enthusiastic help from 'EJ' Trevitt, added a dimension to this book by capturing the ideas of the Slow Movement. Mark added a lightness of touch to the subject matter. At his invitation Carl Honoré, author of *In Praise of Slow*, kindly met us on a couple of occasions to identify the overlap between *Slow Finance* and the Slow Movement more generally. I am also grateful to Tim Dainton, who kindly arranged for Mark Johnstone to visit the Credit Suisse trading floor one morning to get a better understanding of how capital markets worked.

Particular thanks are due to Mary Ziegler. Mary has been at the centre of the book, stitching together many of the different parts into a unified text to form a whole where I can't see the joins. She has been willing to tackle every issue that has arisen, including rewriting the parts where I was failing to make the grade. She has liaised with the academic sources, co-ordinated with the publisher and offered additional content for several gaps. Mary even deferred her progress on her MBA course to ensure she had sufficient time to get this book completed on time. She should rightly be described as a co-writer given her sizable contribution to the book this has become.

Andrew Hunt is quite simply the best economist I have ever come across in my career. I have drawn upon his work liberally in the text and where relevant he has suggested additional sources of information or provided graphical data. He has been willing to talk through my ideas, and where they were a little thin, been willing to say as much. Thank you, Andrew.

I wanted this book to be very relevant to the UK reader. Many of the investment trends identified have been highlighted in a number of different countries. But I need not have worried as the most comprehensive stock market data set, with the longest duration and some of the most insightful studies have come from the London Business School. Professors Elroy Dimson, Paul Marsh and Mike Staunton have been tremendously supportive providing all the detail from their extensive work. In this regard I am grateful to Credit Suisse and the Royal Bank of Scotland for their permission to reproduce the data. I want to highlight and thank Professor Paul Marsh in particular, who read some of the early drafts of the book, and identified areas requiring more work, or facts that challenged some of my conclusions. This was immensely helpful in making the overall book much more robust in terms of its academic content.

I would also like to thank Alistair McDougall of State Street, who compiled the database on the allocations of UK pension funds from the clients of WM over the 25 years to the end of 2010.

Robert Ware of Conygar plc very kindly lent me an office to bring together the team for a 12 week period to get the bulk of the main text complete. This generous offer, and the support of his team including Steven Vaughan and Freddy Jones, meant that I was able to get sufficient momentum on the book to largely hit the publisher's timetable.

Stephen Taylor of Heat Design has brought great ideas to the book on the illustrations. He is highly experienced in the academic book market and has therefore been able bring his knowledge to make the book more pleasurable to open and easier to comprehend.

Nigel Taylor, Ed Stark and Winston Hamill of The Technical People have come together to deliver the App. Nigel and Ed in particular have made it easy for me by taking the idea and delivering, without fuss. Indeed, when they have come up against problems, they have found solutions, and only checked to see I was happy with them. They have also taken on the role of getting the book website, Twitter and Facebook pages up and running too.

Many of the staff at MAM Funds plc have read early drafts of various chapters where I have been concerned whether I have all the facts exactly correct. My particular thanks go to Mark Wright, Simon Wright, James Sullivan and Richard Parfect. They have highlighted specific weaknesses, and offered suggestions for improvement. Martin Turner is also due my thanks since he has been reading texts from early in the project, and his suggestions have helped ensure the book has addressed a full range of issues. I have also had tremendous support and encouragement from the executive board of MAM including Ian Dighe and Graham Hooper.

My former team at Gartmore should also be credited. Although Rob Giles, Adam McConkey, Harmesh Suniara, and Jamie Brooke didn't have any active part in the writing of this book, we worked so effectively together for so many years, that many of the ideas expressed here rely to quite a degree on their investment wisdom.

Over the period of writing I have also had the support of many friends who have come up with suggestions and ideas to make it a richer text. I would like to thank John Edwards, Roddy Monroe, David Nissen, Talithia Williams (my mum), David Pike, Allan Jenkins, and Michael Wills.

Particular thanks are also due to my editor, Lisa Carden.

Finally I would like to thank my family. Although the early parts were written in normal working hours, once I had restarted full time employment the work moved to evenings and weekends. Writing a book is like a slow motion essay crisis, interrupting normal family activities, leaving many routine chores to them whilst I hide away with a keyboard. I am very thankful for their tolerance of my odyssey.

Gervais Williams

Foreword

Some years ago I decided that if I were ever to put pen to paper setting out my investment philosophy and experiences, it would be entitled *Making a Million – Slowly*. Thus I was fascinated and intrigued that the respected fund manager, Gervais Williams – after a lifetime in the City – has entitled his personal contribution *Slow Finance*!

In the Introduction, he talks of personal choices made by heroes and villains, the lucky and the unlucky, and calls on us all to engage more fully with how we allocate our savings. In essence, Gervais' book is an unusual mix of some timely thoughts combined with hard-headed investment conclusions and shrewd advice, honed by his many years of successfully handling his own and other people's savings.

His conclusions very much mirror my own – a focus on 'value', on small rather than large cap stocks, on the importance of dividends and encouragement for the private investor to take an interest in where his fund manager is investing. Where possible, he highlights seeking out investment opportunities closer to home, and points out some of the complexities of investing in far-off economies where valuations are frequently at 'hope and prayer' levels! *Slow Finance* will appeal as much to the hardened professional as to the amateur investor; both should find it enjoyable, challenging and enlightening.

John Lee
Lord Lee of Trafford DL FCA

Introduction

EXPLORING COMPLEX LANDS

'Expect everything, I always say, and the unexpected never happens.'

It could be the motto for anyone trying to cope with the financial crisis of 2008. For anyone who had *expected* the UK housing market to peak out, the stock market to gyrate by around five per cent for several days in succession, or our banks to require emergency funding from the government, then the unexpected never happened.

The line is actually taken from one of my favourite children's books, *The Phantom Tollbooth*,[1] uttered by a curious character called the Whether Man. The Whether Man lives in the Land of Expectations and is just one of many characters the book's hero, a young lad named Milo, encounters on his travels. The story, for those who have not read it, is about Milo's transformation from someone who was initially passive and disinterested in the world of knowledge, into a confident hero who reunites the kingdom of numbers with the kingdom of words after a long period of separation.

In a similar vein, *Slow Finance* is about addressing a separation too; the uneasiness of regular savers who feel apprehensive about how their capital is allocated in an intense world of fast finance and mega-transactions. I do not believe that those outside the financial sector are disinterested or incapable of understanding the world of finance. Far from it. But we do have a 'leave it to the experts' mentality that tends to demote savers and investors to a passive role. *Slow Finance* wants to change this. It seeks to engage readers and investors on key questions regarding the allocation of assets in the future; it seeks to reunite the kingdom of investments with the kingdom of savers.

The story of the recent financial crises is a very emotive affair. Whilst we knew the scale of the financial world was and still is large, few of us realised the risks to our economy when it hit troubled times. For many it was a time of fear, characterised by bank bailouts, business bankruptcies, pay cuts

---

1   Juster, N (2002) *The Phantom Tollbooth* 4th edition, HarperCollins

and job losses. A financial crisis-obsessed media added to the drama. Yet what made the situation all the more difficult was that it was hard to comprehend how it had all come about, particularly for those outside the financial sector. For most, it just seemed impossible to comprehend the scale and complexity of the causes.

In *The Phantom Tollbooth*, there comes a catalyst for change. Milo receives a mysterious package containing a magic tollbooth. The object has the power to transport him to new, extraordinary places where he sees things from new perspectives and meets some most unusual characters. Milo learns some rather valuable life-affirming lessons at the end of his adventures. The ending is, of course, a happy one.

Is there a 'mysterious package' that can help us navigate the daunting world of complex finance? Sadly there is no magic contained in this book, but *Slow Finance* does offer a straightforward outline as to the financial imbalances that have come about. It also has a strong view as to what the future may hold, and why there may be a definite need for behavioural change among capital users and investors to adapt to a new economic universe.

Changing investor behaviour

While change is always disruptive, the good news is that there are some positives that may emerge. *Slow Finance* advocates that readers anticipate how they can take best advantage of the new trends that could emerge in stock markets, by taking a closer interest in how the decisions on asset allocation are made. Is it correct to keep increasing the percentage of our capital invested in fast growth, distant markets? Is it really the case that improved returns can be made by diversifying into equities with good and growing dividend income? Certainly a greater connection between investors and investments would offer many spinoff benefits. In a more uncertain world, shorter and simpler links between investor and investment can only be a good thing. And improving access to capital for domestic companies may grow employment at a time when it may be most needed. New trends like these would re-link the financial sector with the interests of the savers and investors, and the wider purpose of investment.

Slow Finance is a call to action. It is intended to kick-start a debate on how our savings are allocated. After all, the economy is a system that serves us, not vice-versa. We almost need to remind ourselves that the financial world is not ethereal, but depends upon the day-to-day actions of us all. As John Lanchester aptly writes in his book *Whoops!*:

the credit boom. *Slow Finance* highlights how a change in investment values will be reflected in a new trend in portfolio allocation.

The *Slow Finance* App

Smartphones offer the scope to mix the power of analysis with data that is directly relevant to the location of the individual user. The *Slow Finance* App is your tool to identifying the local investment opportunities that may best meet the investors' needs.

The App features:
- Details of the fifty or more quoted businesses that are located closest to the user;
- How well these businesses compare on the Slow Finance attributes;
- The contact details and links to the websites of those most attractive;
- Details of a sell discipline if required;
- An ability to store the details of those that might be most interesting, so that they can be easily reviewed in the future.

Of course, there are no 'silver bullets' in the investment world, so the *Slow Finance* App is an information source, a starting point, a way of recognising and celebrating the success of many local quoted businesses. Decisions on investment matters are solely the responsibility of the individual or their advisors.

Who is this book for?

Slow Finance has been written for those who are interested in what may drive the coming change in financial trends. There is plenty in this book that is controversial. Some may choose to interpret the evidence in a different way or argue against the conclusions. For these reasons it may be of specific interest to students, academics and indeed anyone interested in addressing the UK's position in the global economy.

Slow Finance is an invitation to everyone to more fully engage in an informed and considered conversation on how we allocate our savings. As economist John Kay said: 'The real issues of economics are vital and fascinating, and raise some of the most important social and political questions of our time.'[3]

---

3   Kay, J (2004) *The Truth about Markets: Why Some Countries Are Rich and Others Are Poor*, Penguin, p. 1.

This book is particularly relevant for savers and investors, especially those who feel they would like to have a greater impact on how their capital is allocated. For the private saver or those with a Self-Invested Personal Pension (SIPP) with an interest in the economy, this book may provide an explanation of how financial trends have unfolded in the past, and through this, offer some insight into how trends might change in the future. For both savers and private investors, the App might be an interesting way of engaging with local quoted businesses. For experienced investors, *Slow Finance* summarises the magnitude of some of the most sustained premium performance trends in past decades.

There is an apocryphal story from Ireland. A holiday motorist is lost in the lanes of Donegal and sees a local farmer beside the lane. He stops and asks his way, and the farmer replies, 'Now if you want to get there, you wouldn't be wanting to start from here.' And so it is with the financial sector. But we have to start from where we are. There is no value in deliberating as to how things may have been different had the investment world or governments acted differently. The scale of past financial trends is history. Whatever happens next, starts from here.

For most living through the current economic climate, there is a nagging worry: the financial world seems to be making money out of thin air, whilst the underlying UK economy appears to be fragile. This book has been written to address that dichotomy. The investment world has always dealt with risk, but with more austere times ahead, achieving an attractive investment return may be more challenging.

The *Phantom Tollbooth* analogy illustrates that the world of economics is a story like any other. Our decisions are based on our perceptions and willingness to engage with the issues. The financial world is extraordinarily varied, but still firmly rooted on the choices made by individuals; of heroes and villains, the lucky and the unlucky. It is a world *Slow Finance* explores in more detail. If the financial trends are changing, then it is more important than ever to have an opinion. If we are to '*expect everything*', then it is doubly important to take a bold view on these issues. Just how relevant are the ideas in *Slow Finance*? I'll leave you to answer that question.

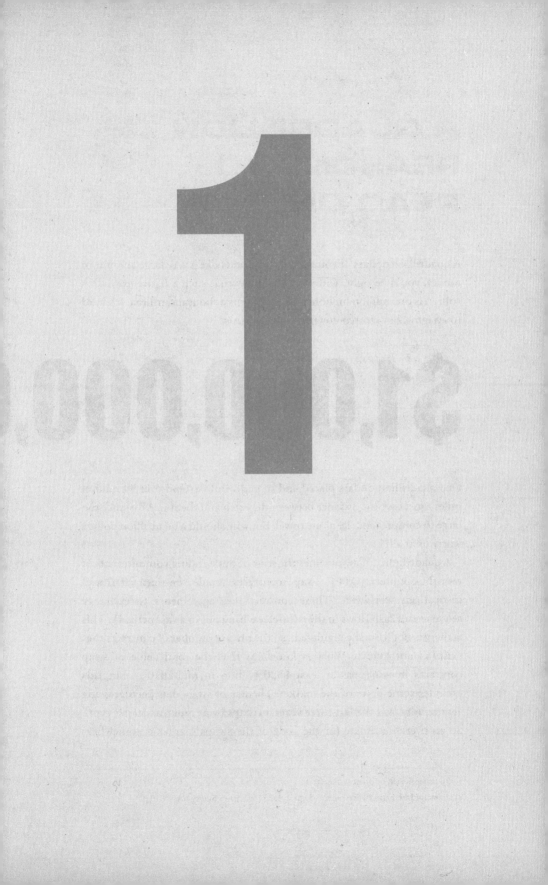

A QUADRILLION REASONS TO READ ON

A quadrillion dollars. If you think that sounds like a very large amount of money, you'd be right. Did you even know that such a figure existed? A trillion is one million million; a quadrillion is a thousand trillion. It's hard to imagine, but written down it looks like this:

One quadrillion dollars placed end to end would extend over 94 million miles – just over the distance between the earth and the sun. A distance too large to comprehend, let alone travel. But why should a quadrillion dollars worry us at all?

A quadrillion dollars outlines the scale of outstanding commitments of over-the-counter (OTC) swap contracts made between financial institutions worldwide. These contracts are agreements to exchange sequences of cash flows in the future, reaching out in a vast network. This activity is not formally regulated,[1] so the precise number of contracts that exists is not known. What is known is that the total value of swap contracts in issue was at least $580 trillion in mid-2010[2] – but this excludes some parts of the market. The use of swaps has been growing very rapidly over the last three years, perhaps by as much as 50 per cent.[3] So an overall estimate for the scale of the swaps market is somewhere

---

1   In either the UK or US as at May 2011
2   Bank for International Settlements Semi-Annual Derivatives Survey June 2010 p. 1
3   ISDA

between $580 trillion and $1 quadrillion.[4] And if past trends persist, outstanding commitments will certainly stretch past the one quadrillion dollar mark in time.

Financial commitments of this scale have come about as we try to manage risk in a connected world. As the financial sector has grown, relationships that were once relatively straightforward have become more complex and opaque. The orientation of the financial sector has become increasingly skewed towards large and international. As a result, the links between savers, the original providers of capital, and the financial markets, which allocate that capital, have become less coherent. The two have grown apart and become more disconnected. Within the financial services industry, disconnects exist at other levels too. National financial regulators

00,000,000

are disempowered by the scale of international capital flows and legal structures designed to maintain exemption from local laws.[5]

These issues are not just academic concerns. The global financial network is gigantic, so large that it overshadows the tangible activities taking place in our economy. And however disconnected we may feel as individuals from the financial sector, it is still closely reliant on everyone in one key area. When the financial sector has periodic crises, taxpayers and users of financial services are the ones that are required to resolve the imbalances.

The trend towards rapid financial expansion has been in place so long that it appears that it will continue without end. How is it that the financial markets have grown as far and as fast as they have, and how might they fare if debt became scarce again? Can we anticipate how investment behaviour might change? And what can individual investors do to best protect their savings?

---

4   Office of the Comptroller of the Currency Quarterly Report on Bank Derivatives Activities Q42010

5   Plender, P in *Financial Times* 04.05.2011 *ET stokes fears about sweeping swaps rules* p. 30

Fig 1.1: What size means

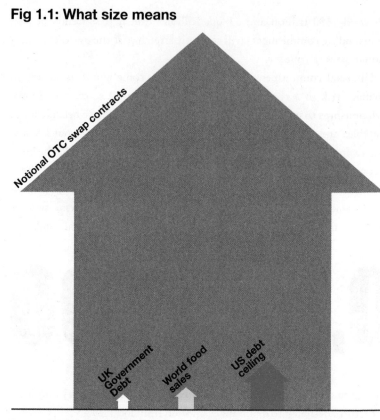

Source: Bank for International Settlements, International Monetary Fund,
UK Debt Management Agency

Fueling finance: innovation, deregulation and globalisation

In the last two-and-a-half decades there has been extraordinary growth in the UK financial sector – far faster than in many other industries. In that period the sector has grown in size from just over 18 per cent of the economy to nearer 25 per cent.[6] The globalisation of trade and capital flows, looser regulation and more competition between the banks have created perfect conditions for the sector to grow. This unbridled growth is positive in some respects. The UK financial sector is a successful, world-class industry, providing many jobs, with the consequent tax take funding

---

6   Anastassova-Chirmiciu, L (2008) *The Evolution of UK and London Employment Rates* Greater London Authority Economics pp. 26–28

Fig 1.2: Comprehending distance

One quadrillion dollars stretch from the
earth to the sun (93,000,000 miles)

One hundred lunar expeditions
(48,000,000 miles)

One thousand round trips
London to Sydney
(21,300,000 miles)

One thousand round trips Lands End
to John O'Groats
(1,748,000 miles)

a good proportion of the public purse. But how does the City manage to generate such high levels of profit, especially in recent times when the rest of the economy appears to be struggling to make any headway?

Before the 1990s, economic growth was normally characterised by periods of boom and bust – an economy accelerating, becoming unbalanced when certain elements such as the financial sector became overheated, then stabilisers clicked in and the imbalances were addressed. The Bank of England used interest rates as a mechanism to choke off demand for credit, with the prospect of encouraging borrowing again when the economy slowed too much. But over the last 25 years this has changed. Inflation peaked at 7.5 per cent in 1991,[7] and it has fallen steadily since then. Aside from the period when the pound shadowed the European Exchange Rate Mechanism up to 1992, interest rates have fallen to lower and lower levels. In early 2011, the UK base

---

7   Office for National Statistics, Consumer Prices Index Annualised, Series D70E

rate[8] has reached an exceptionally low 0.5 per cent – the lowest since the Bank of England was founded in 1694.[9]

The globalisation of capital flows and the traded goods sector has played a key role in this. It made it possible to take greater advantage of lower cost of production in other parts of the world, bringing cheaper and cheaper imported goods into the UK. While the cost of rent or other services rose sharply, the overall measure of UK inflation has stayed subdued, allowing interest rates to stay relatively low.[10]

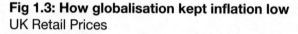

Fig 1.3: How globalisation kept inflation low
UK Retail Prices

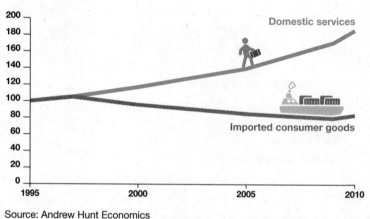

Source: Andrew Hunt Economics

At the same time, deregulation and innovation enhanced London's status as a major international financial centre. London brought together capital surpluses with novel investment products developed in western markets, such as the US and the UK. It did not matter that local savings rates were falling given the strong capital flows from overseas. This trend helped maintain a steady flow of low-cost finance; the foundation for a long period of economic growth.

---

8 UK base rate: Reference lending rate paid by the Bank of England on commercial bank reserves

9 Bank of England Monetary Policy Committee

10 Even when the official interest rates did rise a little, the longer-term trend of falling interest rates on 10-year bonds helped keep the positive economic trend going through the period

'The period between 1992 and 2007 brought probably the best years of economic development that the world has ever seen'.[11]

Professor Charles Goodhart, London School of Economics

London's near-unique role, with historic connections to emerging economies, its well-developed financial community and the fact it had been released from its previously parochial industry structure by deregulation, meant that it could take the lead as global financial trade accelerated. London became more connected with the rapid growth of the emerging markets, rather than remaining constrained by the more modest growth of the UK economy. Applied technology helped step up the pace at which financial transactions could be arranged and carried out. But the financial sector would never have grown to its current scale without a sea-change in the scale and availability of credit.

Rush: the impact of credit

Easy credit has the effect of a sugar rush on the financial sector. Plentiful credit brings forward economic activity, facilitating growth in the near-term. Faster economic growth helps businesses to record larger profits, and share prices to rise. Speculation on share prices or house prices offers quick profits, particularly in an environment where more participants make it easier to buy and sell assets. Plentiful credit favours the imprudent over the prudent, as the more debt is used, the greater the potential gains. Rapid growth in debt effectively fuels asset prices in a positive feedback loop.

In the fifty years prior to 1986, credit grew broadly in line with GDP, expanding modestly in real terms. But after 1986, credit growth took off, since banks had rebuilt their balance sheets after the problems of over-exposure to sovereign debt. With modest government or third-party regulation in some of the newer products, and the positive financial environment at the time, they felt encouraged to lend more progressively in domestic markets. This led to rises in all asset prices and the arrival by the 1980s of a 'loadsamoney' generation.

In 1985, the average home cost just over £33,000. By the market peak in 2007, that price had risen over 500 per cent, as the ability to borrow drove up the price homebuyers were willing to pay for a property.[12] Those with

---

11 Goodheart, C *(2009) in Banking Crisis: Dealing with the Failure of the UK Banks* (2009) Treasury Select Committee, Seventh Report of Session 2008-09 p. 31 House of Commons

12 Nationwide House Price Index 1975-2010 Inflation Adjusted

mortgages of 80 or 90 per cent on the price of their homes frequently made a capital gain many times the scale of their original deposit on the house in just a few of years. This had spillover effects; higher house prices and a shift in attitudes to debt encouraged homeowners to keep moving, borrowing larger sums each time to climb the housing ladder. Others used the house price increases to remortgage, and spend new-found gains through the economy. The consumer boom led to more low-cost imports, keeping inflation modest even though a full scale credit boom had begun. Aside from a brief period in the early 1990s[13], the trends of the next 25 years were established. By 2007, the money owed on mortgages, loans and credit cards far outweighed what the UK economy produced in a year. Asset values were increasingly disconnected from average earnings of a UK employee.

Fig 1.4: The UK housing bubble
House price £

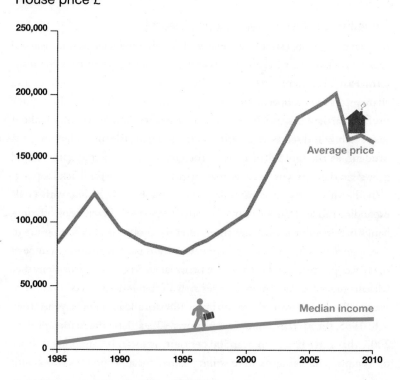

Data: Nationwide, Office for National Statistics

---

13 Ending with sterling's ejection from the European Exchange Rate Mechanism in 1992

'Plentiful debt, made possible by progressively lower inflation rates, transformed the financial landscape and fuelled the extraordinary scaling up of all sorts of money markets'

Gervais Williams

Over the 25 years of the credit boom, the UK debt markets have evolved in sophistication. The most significant trend has been the surge in marketable debt. Previously when banks lent to customers, they generally did so using money from their own balance sheets. If anything went wrong, the banks took the pain. But during the last 25 years, this practice has changed. Banks frequently arrange the borrowing for corporate customers, but more frequently tend to sell these debts on to other investors. The government has long followed a similar process, selling its debt in the form of Gilts or government bonds. Pension and insurance funds liked buying corporate debt since it paid a slightly higher rate of interest than Gilts.

The mark of success or otherwise evolved from being the ultimate repayment of the loan, to the first market price on the debt following the deal. If the price moved to a premium in the aftermarket, the issue was seen as a success and financiers quickly moved on to the next deal. Attitudes evolved. There was scope for debt traders to buy and sell debt for a quick profit. The concept of patient capital was replaced by a growing number of impatient investors. Falling inflation rates lead to the bond markets rising year after year, and therefore traders were able to keep booking decent trading profits every year. The liquidity in these markets meant that investors no longer needed to concern themselves too much with the risk on the underlying borrower, as they were able to take profits on the trend of falling interest rates. It did not pay to be too responsible. The growth in the availability of credit meant that even those who perhaps would have struggled to repay loans were bailed out by the trend of falling interest rates and rising value of assets. Everyone was a winner.

With the new forms of debt, novel products were developed. While these products increased in scale and complexity, the plan was to match different loans so that the risks of default in one type of loan would be offset by others that continued to service their interest payments, so that the default risk of the overall product was reduced. Collateralised Debt Obligations (CDOs) allowed loans from different types of lenders (home mortgages, corporate loans and credit cards, for example) to be pooled in a single investment fund, and then sold as part of a package to investors. (See

Appendix 1.) By the mid-2000s these products were so popular that even those who were overstretched could continue to borrow, repaying their earlier commitments along the way. Within the CDO structure, even investors in the most risky assets appeared to be sheltered from loan defaults. The novelty of the model contributed to the view that the financial sector was making the system safer through genuine innovation, spreading credit risk more widely between institutions and non-financial investors. In fact, complex, tiered relationships simply concealed the true nature of the risks.

Layering disconnection

Towards the end of 2005 I became concerned that the credit boom had reached a point where it was inevitable that the trend could no longer be sustained. At this stage global debt was being issued so fast that it was difficult to find enough customers willing to borrow. This led to CDOs being recycled through the creation of new CDOs. Financial products were aggregated into new CDOs, known as CDOs Squared – financial products not backed by real loans, but made up of the cashflows derived from them. This represented not one layer of leverage and disconnection, but sometimes as many as four[14]. In some ways the financial sector had already over-optimised the structure of its lending through these funds. Now it was doing so again, but with less room for error each time. In these structures, the capital 'safety margin' was engineered to be wafer-thin.

Japan had been using Quantitative Easing (QE) (see Appendix 2) in an attempt to stimulate its economy over the 1990s, creating electronic money to buy government bonds and other assets, to lubricate the financial system. By the middle of the 2000s, world economic growth was so strong that the Bank of Japan felt the QE policy could be reversed. I was unsure whether this change would overwhelm the safety margin of the CDO structures and end the credit boom. I thought there was a good chance that it would. Although the financial markets wobbled during 2006, my fears proved premature. But by May 2007, with commodity prices rising fast as world growth accelerated, bond yields started to rise – and the credit boom came to an abrupt halt as the increased cost of borrowing[15] eroded the headroom built into some of the sophisticated financial debt products.

---

14 Barnett-Hart, A K (2009) *The Story of the CDO Market Meltdown: An Empirical Analysis*, Harvard College

15 Even via the CDO structure

In the US there is close linkage between bond prices and the cost of mortgage payments. Sub-prime borrowers[16] were already struggling to meet interest payments and began to default. It was assumed that CDOs diluted risk by spreading it over a larger group of investors. But it soon became clear that the CDO model was flawed. The risk of default had not been contained through a tiered structure, as had been envisaged. In fact, some risks were concentrated through interrelated cash flows drawn from other layers of borrowing.

Given that this structure had become a popular method of financing at the time, many institutions tried to reduce their CDO holdings simultaneously. Some CDOs were so complex that many investors were unable to work out the true nature of the assets that they held. Documents outlining some structures ran to many hundreds of pages and there were specific factors that could push an investment over a performance 'cliff'.[17] These features led to uncertainty over what the right price for these assets really was. A powerful negative cycle began. Within a year, credit markets had all but frozen up.

Credit instability

'You have to avoid debt because debt makes the system more fragile. You have to increase redundancies in some spaces. You have to avoid optimisation.'

Nassim Taleb, The Black Swan:
The Impact of the Highly Improbable[18]

A healthy financial system is the backbone of a healthy economy. However rapid credit growth is inherently unstable. One person's 'cash in' means someone else's 'cash out'.[19] Credit involves making judgments – about how 'safe' the person on the other side is, and about the true value of the asset against which the lending is secured. They both change over time, sometimes abruptly.

Traditionally central banks have managed the risks of instability within the financial system by monitoring the risk within it. Normally as the financial sector overheats, the central bank steps in and puts up interest rates. In extreme times, they act as Lender of Last Resort – giving credit to

---

16 Sub-prime: Borrowers perceived to be of greater risk of default, and therefore offered more costly debt financing above the prime rate

17 Where changes in the performance of an underlying asset would be amplified

18 *Financial Times* 04.05.2011

19 Minsky, P (2008) *Stabilizing an Unstable Economy*, McGraw-Hill Professional

banks at critical times when no one else will. But in the last 25 years, this role has become *less* significant; globalisation led to cheaper imports that offset other inflationary costs in the economy. So this time, in spite of the financial sector becoming overheated, a progressive fall in the rate of inflation inhibited central banks from stepping in to end the credit bubble. Households, companies and governments all drew heavily on the debt markets after 1986, creating perhaps the largest credit bubble of all time.

All banks use short-term deposits to fund their liabilities. In 2007, many had a relatively small proportion of retail deposits, and were using wholesale funding to finance long-term strategies. As perceptions about their safety changed, banks were forced to pay higher and higher interest rates to keep investors funding their debts overnight. Depositors became concerned about the security of their savings, and withdrew from lending to banks paying the highest overnight interest rates. Long queues developed outside Northern Rock, as customers sought to withdraw their savings too in the first run on a UK bank since 1878. It's all an illustration of how quickly financial crises can arrive. There is a City saying that recovery looks like a set of stairs, whereas a financial crisis looks more like a lift shaft.

Fig 1.5: The scale of the credit boom
US Credit Market Debt 1929-2010
(% nominal US GDP)

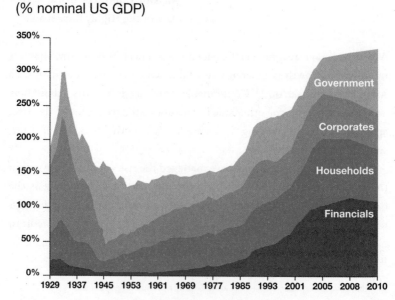

Source: Morgan Stanley Research/Bloomberg/International Monetary Fund

After a credit boom of this size, with the overall scale of debt in issue being far from the long term norm, it is no surprise that a severe recession followed the credit crunch; much worse than the downturns of the early 1980s or the early 1990s.[20]

The disconnect widens

Of greater concern, regulators and governments faced the potential collapse of the entire financial system. For many around the world, livelihoods, homes, savings or pensions and prospects for future investments were all at stake. The scale of the risks triggered some extraordinary actions. The Bank of England made confidential loans of more than 60 billion pounds to the banks, and the government extended explicit guarantees, changing the ground rules in the financial sector.[21]

Central banks have always been seen as Lenders of Last Resort – the ones that can step in, offering finance to banks when money flows around the system have dried up. It is a critical financial and societal role, as no one wants the safety of the savings held in commercial banks to be in question. At the height of the credit crisis, central banks moved beyond that role to guarantee the operation of some money markets, providing what is known as liquidity.[22] Central banks were no longer Lenders of Last Resort. They became, in effect, Dealers of Last Resort. This meant stepping over a psychological line, to ensure that the liquidity in some parts of the financial markets continued.

The purpose of this was to ensure that the differences between prices in different parts of the money markets did not become too great. The price of some securities had fallen to abnormally low levels, and the amount lent was dependent upon the value of those securities. There was a danger that the pricing anomalies would cause some financial institutions to be asked to repay some of their previous borrowings made when the prices were much higher, with ready money they now did not have. To do nothing would have led to these institutions being declared insolvent. If their portfolios were then sold too, the pricing anomalies would have become even more extreme. Left unchecked, this process could have caused the progressive failure of the financial system.

---

20 Bloomberg *IMF Cuts Global Forecast on Worst Crisis Since 1930s* on 02.04.2011
21 Mervyn King, Governor of the Bank of England, reported on BBC 24.11.09
22 Liquidity: Marketability or degree to which an asset can be bought or sold

But the risks and rewards of this new policy do not fall equally on banks and other financial institutions. The central bank 'guarantee of market liquidity' cannot back all financial markets simultaneously. The Bank of England had to prioritise those asset markets relevant to the banks where the public has high-street deposits. These favoured high street banks were able to address their liquidity problems, irrespective of the level of their financial imprudence. They had, in effect, been allowed to disconnect from the implications of their actions. Central banks now appear to be playing two conflicting roles simultaneously. They are committed to overseeing financial stability, yet have also set precedents in a way that exacerbates instability.[23]

The most serious consequence of this role shift is that parts of the financial sector seem to have become even further removed from the normal disciplines of the real world. In spite of the recent financial scare, many banks have resumed many of their earlier activities and with renewed gusto, fuelled by the boost to financial liquidity injected by QE.

As the government has extended its financial commitments, the amount that it needs to borrow each year has grown at an extraordinary pace, increasing five times over between 2006 and 2009.[24]

The scale of intervention via QE is dramatic. Despite the much larger amount of debt the UK government has issued, the Bank of England bought most of it itself in 2009/10 via QE. It has now bought almost 200 billion pounds of UK government debt, just under 20 per cent of all the Gilts in issue.[25] For me, this marks the final phase of the recent credit boom.

The UK economy needed this scale of injection of financial liquidity to get the financial system restarted. Even with these huge sums, the UK economy is barely growing.[26] But now that the 2008 crisis has passed, many people may not realise that the disconnections in the financial sector have not disappeared. They have grown. Many parts of the global economy are bloated with debt, but QE has injected life into asset markets. This is why, in my view, the UK stock market recovered to almost pre-crisis levels by the end of 2010. The City appears as though it has been able to get back to business very quickly, apparently disconnected from the difficulties in the rest of the economy.

---

23 Merhling, P (2010) *The New Lombard Street: How the Fed became the Dealer of Last Resort*, Princeton University Press

24 UK Debt Management Office (2010) Quarterly Review

25 UK Debt Management Office Central Government Net Cash Requirement

26 Reuters, 27th April 2011 *FTSE swings higher on UK GDP relief, corporate earnings*

Fig 1.6: How much cash does the UK government need?
Central Government Net Cash Requirement (£bn)

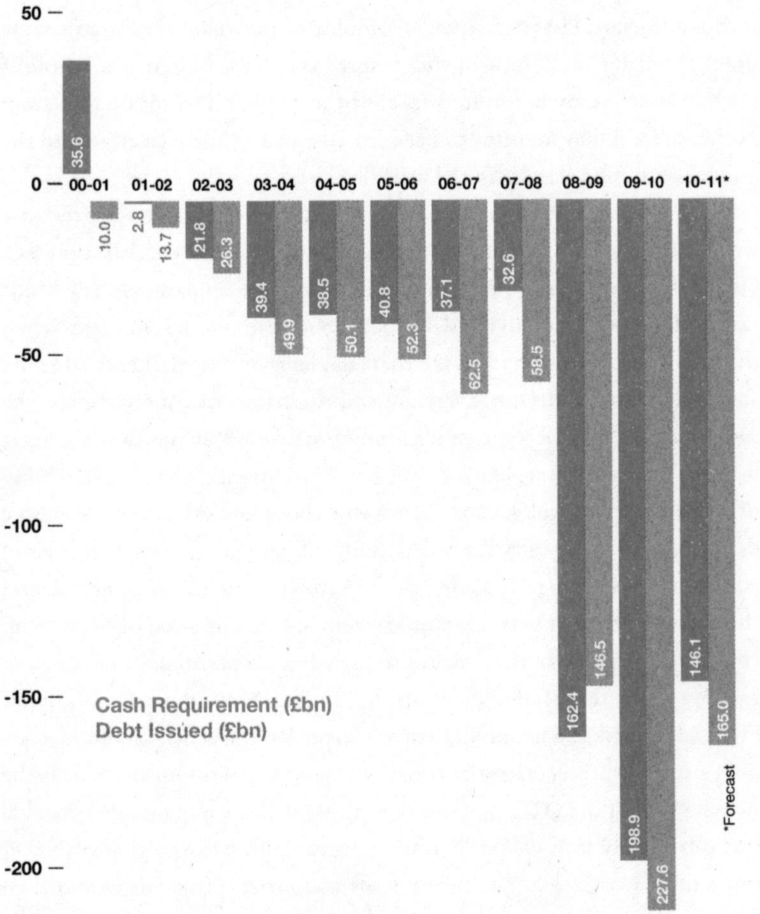

Year	Cash Requirement (£bn)	Debt Issued (£bn)
00-01	35.6	10.0
01-02	2.8	13.7
02-03	21.8	26.3
03-04	39.4	49.9
04-05	38.5	50.1
05-06	40.8	52.3
06-07	37.1	62.5
07-08	32.6	58.5
08-09	162.4	227.6
09-10	146.5	198.9
10-11*	146.1	165.0

Cash Requirement (£bn)
Debt Issued (£bn)

*Forecast

Source: UK Debt Management Office, 2010

Bank-to-bank transactions

Cutting interest rates to very low levels and injecting extra capital into the financial markets with QE has boosted many financial activities. This includes trades that take place directly between banks, including those outside regulated exchanges – described as 'over-the-counter' (OTC).[27] The

---

27 OTC trades include trades in a wide range of financial instruments, including stocks, bonds, currencies and other structures derived from those assets (derivatives)

OTC market allows banks to carry out private transactions with each other. (See Appendix 3.)

The OTC swap market is considered by most participants to be intrinsically safe. But the market is complex, not formally regulated and, as highlighted at the opening of this chapter, very large indeed. The whole of the world economy amounted to $58tn in 2009.[28] The total OTC swap positions held may amount to between 10 and 17 times the size of all the annual economic activity in the world!

In my view, the liquidity of the swaps market is heavily related to the ease with which credit can be accessed. And yet we also know that the policy of QE cannot be expanded indefinitely. The Bank of England already holds just under one fifth of all the debt the UK Government has in issue. When the financial lubrication from QE that enables the swap markets to operate smoothly starts to dry up, there are real uncertainties. At that stage, the swaps market may become more limited in scope.[29] If the swaps market dries up, then corporate loans will be harder to finance, and the availability of corporate credit will decline. Worse still, those loans that mature may be difficult to roll over into new loans, and will need to be repaid, at least in part. This could bring the alchemy of the credit boom to a formal end, and the years of credit constraint would begin. Given the scale of OTC swap contracts, the effect of the unwinding could be substantial.

Many of the financial institutions holding OTC swap positions are not high-street banks. With no high-street deposits, the central bank has few obligations to protect them at times of financial stress. For me, this is the Achilles heel of the OTC swap market. There will always be some financial institutions holding swaps that are vulnerable to becoming insolvent at times of market stress. The counterparties to their positions would then find that their positions were unmatched, and the accumulated profits or losses would need to be recognised immediately.[30] If this occurred at a time when market conditions were uncertain, the unexpected losses could spill over to other institutions and threaten their solvency too. This kind of risk is called systemic risk – risk within the system itself. Given the scale of the

---

28 World Bank Statistics GDP (2009) p. 4

29 Lending institutions need the swap to be available at a fine bid/offer spread, in a liquid market and in large scale – ideally in all three areas (currency/ interest rates and CDSs) – to successfully make the loans.

30 Dependent on previous collateral transfers. Institutions with a notional profit would become a claimant on the counterparty's assets

Fig 1.7: How the financial sector has outgrown the underlying economy
Over The Counter Swap Trades, (US$ bn)

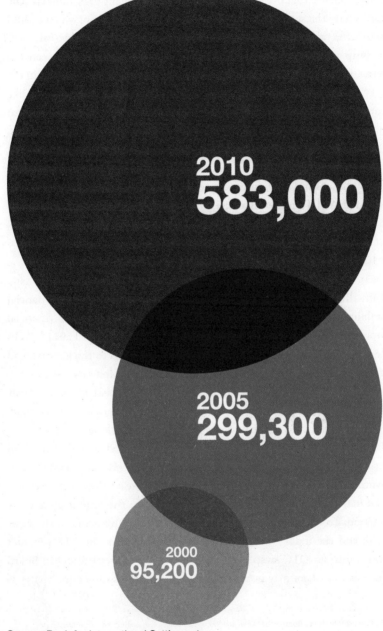

2010
583,000

2005
299,300

2000
95,200

Source: Bank for International Settlements

OTC positions, a loss of just one tenth of 1 per cent of the whole market would amount to a very considerable loss, compared with the capital reserves of the banking system.

The scenario that I've just painted is believed by many to be unlikely. The banks have the security of the assets held against the swap, which should match the value of the contract to a large degree. On top of this, variances in swap values are frequently made up by cash payments between the relevant parties. But I am not reassured. Many of the assets involved in the OTC swap markets are no longer easily tradable financial instruments like currency. Many are corporate loans. Clearly these are more difficult to trade in a troubled market, and there is greater scope for sizable losses. During the 2008 crisis remarkably few businesses went bankrupt, following the substantial cut in interest rates reducing the costs of many corporate loans at that time. With interest rates at record lows, that effect cannot be repeated. And if another financial crisis occurred in the future, the scope of central banks to react is constrained by the scale of QE already undertaken.

How Exchange Traded Funds have evolved

With this in mind, it is unsettling to see a warning from the Financial Stability Board, which co-ordinates bank regulators, about financial innovation in Exchange Traded Funds (ETFs), issued in April 2011.[31] ETFs began as straightforward, 'vanilla' products, designed to track a financial index. They offer investors the advantage of relatively low-cost exposure to a range of assets, and the ability to trade those assets continuously throughout the day. Initially these funds were relatively easy to understand, since they held a list of the underlying shares of the relevant index.

But now the Financial Stability Board has warned that the financial structure of some ETFs has evolved to something that is rather different. Synthetic ETFs take the cash from investors and use it to buy an investment that may not be directly related to the index that the fund is apparently offering. To make up the difference in the price movements of the asset held, and the index that the investor is buying into, the ETF provider enters into an OTC swap agreement. But the Financial Stability Board believes that there may be an issue here. 'Since the swap counterparty is

---

31 Financial Stability Board (2011) *Potential financial stability issues arising from recent trends in Exchange-Traded Funds (ETFs)* 12.04.11

typically the bank also acting as ETF provider,' its report states, 'investors may be exposed if the bank defaults. Therefore, problems at those banks that are most active in swap-based ETFs may constitute a powerful source of contagion and systemic risk.'[32]

If issues arise, investors in the ETF may not be able to sell such assets at anything like the value of the underlying index that they were hoping to track, if they are able to do so at all. ETFs offer a route for banks to get cash in, against an asset that, although marketable, could prove difficult to sell, even in more regular markets. The structures carry greater risks than investors may appreciate.

ETFs have grown very rapidly over recent years, and the overall amount in issue is just over $1 trillion, or $1 million million. Over the last few years there have been very sizable inflows into ETFs, so the need to liquidate underlying assets has not been tested. However, at some stage financial markets are likely to peak and then decline, perhaps as QE comes to an end, or maybe as inflationary pressures rise. At these times, it is plausible that many ETF investors may seek to withdraw their capital when underlying liquidity is more limited than in recent years. The withdrawal of capital from ETFs at a time when markets might be falling would be problematic.[33] If ETF redemptions were very large, it could precipitate the liquidation of a bank. The situation is made more complex by the use of debt in some ETFs – leveraged ETFs – that use borrowing to amplify market movements.

What conclusions can be drawn from this? Firstly, the scale of the OTC swap market is uncomfortably large when compared to the overall scale of general economic activity. Complex relationships of this scale are fundamentally unsound because of the low tolerance to errors. Looking back to the issues that emerged in the CDO analysis by Anna Barnett-Hart of Harvard College is illuminating.[34] She believes that the key is to unravel complexity to a point where investors can make informed decisions again.

Secondly, it is likely that the financial sector will face major challenges again. Novel structures have taken stable financial products and made them more financially efficient. There is ample scope for the 'market

---

32 Financial Stability Board (2011) *Potential financial stability issues arising from recent trends in Exchange-Traded Funds (ETFs)* p. 6 12.04.11

33 In this scenario, the ETF provider would be unable to raise capital from the sale of the illiquid underlying asset in the ETF, and it is likely their own balance sheet would be under liquidity constraints to meet all the other liabilities they may have.

34 Barnett-Hart, A K (2009) *The Story of the CDO Market Meltdown: An Empirical Analysis*, Harvard College

imperfections, misaligned incentives, and human excesses'[35] seen in the CDO crisis to reappear, possibly in the ETF market or elsewhere in the swaps area. Volatility can change very rapidly indeed now that it is possible to initiate and process trades in nanoseconds,[36] whilst it can take days to fully appreciate the exact exposure to derivatives counterparties.[37] The conclusion must be that some financial structures, which may be appropriate in modest scale and in the right context, may have grown too large relative to the real economy, and too sophisticated since a large part of the margin of safety has been engineered out too. In the financial sector, this issue seems to appear and re-appear with some regularity.

The route from here

It is now time to look beyond the present, to try to establish what might happen when current economic trends come to an end. Once the overall buy-in of government debt under QE comes to an end, we will enter a period of greater financial realism. Given that credit growth has brought forward economic growth and led to the rise in the asset markets, a reverse of this trend would be a major change. As established trends change, our habits as investors can be expected to evolve to reflect the new reality.

The UK government is burdened with almost £1 trillion of debt.[38] That's £1,000,000,000,000. Our spending commitments grew rapidly when government receipts were high. Government receipts have fallen back, but government outgoings through unemployment benefit, for example, are near impossible to change. Even with interest rates low, paying the interest alone on UK government debt costs almost £42bn a year[39] – more than the entire education budget. Many UK households are also overextended in terms of debt. This becomes more problematic if assets like houses have peaked in value.

There is now broad agreement that the government mismatch between income and expenditure should be addressed, to bring it down to a figure closer to a long-term average. A reduced willingness to borrow implies that

35 Barnett-Hart, A K (2009) *The Story of the CDO Market Meltdown: An Empirical Analysis*, Harvard College

36 The Economist *Rise of the machines:Algorithmic trading causes concern among investors and regulators* 30.07.09

37 The Economist *The uses and abuses of mathematical models* 11.02.11

38 UK Debt Management Office

39 The Guardian *UK Debt Interest bill will rise to £70bn without action, says David Cameron* Monday 7.06.10

households and governments face a period of austerity. Economist Andrew Hunt believes that households in the US and the UK will have to spend around 4 to 6 per cent *less* in GDP terms in order to rebalance effectively.[40] This shift could slow the growth of the UK economy quite substantially. These changes will affect us all – in how much tax we have to pay, and as users of the health service and schools, for example. And even if the government is successful in meeting its plans to reduce expenditure, it will still remain higher than government income, and the overall scale of government borrowing will continue to rise.

With austerity budgets being introduced across most of the developed economies simultaneously in the coming years, and the artificial 'medicine' of QE no longer being increased, it seems obvious that the UK economy cannot continue to deliver past levels of growth. We need to recognise the risk that developed economies are entering a period of slow economic momentum. It does not mean that the UK economy will not grow at all, or that there will not be areas of dynamism. But overall, I describe this period rather simplistically as 'ex-growth'. It's a time that will be particularly challenging for investors who have become accustomed to debt-driven increases in asset prices.

The recession of 2008/09 demonstrated that the growth of the financial sector is a secular trend that has limits. There are ingrained habits in place that have been optimised for an environment characterised by ample credit. As QE comes to an end, the financial sector will enter a new period – an era of credit constraint. We should expect market liquidity to decline, undermining the operation of some parts of the financial world, particularly those strategies that are heavily dependent on frequent transactions to generate a return. While this might be accepted in concept by many, there is little urgency to change as long as uptrends persist. After all, it is impossible to accurately anticipate extreme events, or plan for every outlier.[41]

Whilst there is little to be gained by trying to finesse the timing, or identify the exact catalyst of the change, the evidence suggests that the previous trends will end. Given the scale of that change when it comes, it is more than sensible for investors to plan ahead. Perhaps a more considered approach – indeed a slower approach – is needed now.

---

40 Hunt, A (2011) *Investment Review – Life on Mars?* 14.04.2010 Andrew Hunt Economics

41 Taleb, N N (2008) *The Black Swan: The Impact of the Highly Improbable*, Penguin

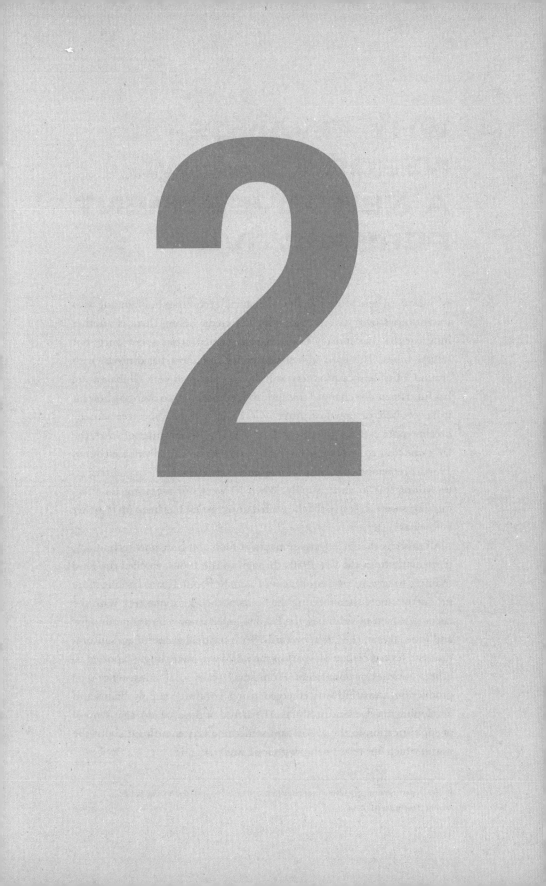

WHY FINANCE NEEDS TO SLOW: A NEW INVESTMENT PERSPECTIVE

We have been here before. While the financial sector may be grappling with uncertainties over its direction after the credit boom, there is another industry that has already been through similar crises – not once, but several times. The food industry supplies our most basic needs, with around $4 trillion of products[1] sold by retailers each year. Globalisation has fundamentally changed this industry, but it is easy to overlook how far it has evolved, or how fast. After World War II, food shortages actually became more extreme for a period. As recently as the winter of 1947, the UK came close to starvation. Food rationing was only finally phased out in 1954.[2] I remember my father explaining that although he was a farmer, everything was in short supply. When he went out rabbiting for food, cartridges were so scarce that he waited until two rabbits lined up together before having a shot.

All this has changed. Developments in food and transport technology, particularly from the late 1950s through to the 1980s, enabled the food industry to have its own equivalent of a credit boom. Farms became more productive, more than meeting the needs of their local markets. With the encouragement of subsidies, the EU developed its own butter mountains and wine lakes in the 1980s onwards. With regional excess of agricultural produce, food grown in one part of the world was increasingly exported to other countries or continents. From small scale, local, subsistence-type production, a vast industry emerged, using worldwide supply chains and developing novel, exotic products. The arrival of the avocado, that symbol of sophistication in the 1970s, said something very significant about the way in which our relationship with food was changing.

---

1   US Department of Agriculture Economic Research *Global Food Market Briefing* 2010

2   BBC *On this day* 04.07.54

Of course, the evolution of the food industry has many obvious benefits. Western populations now have access to a much larger range of products, many available out of season, sourced from around the globe. Our supermarkets are fully stocked with every food consumers might want to buy. Food manufacturers have integrated different ingredients together to offer ready-to-eat finished products. And the cost of food relative to our wages has fallen by a sizable degree over the last 40 years.

Fig 2.1: Eating at the family budget
UK Real food prices

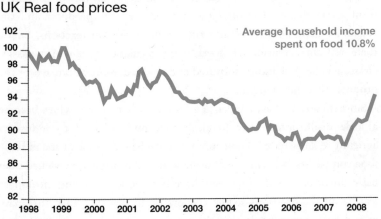

Average household income spent on food 10.8%

Source: Living Costs & Food Survey, Office for National Statistics; Defra Food Statistics Pocketbook

But these benefits have come at a cost. The globalisation of food production has created new problems. As individuals progressively buy more food products rather than raw ingredients, the greater the element of control ceded to the food manufacturer. As agriculture has become industrialised, individuals have become more disconnected from the meal on their plates.

'Eating is an agricultural act. ... Most eaters are, however, no longer aware that this is true. They think of food as an agricultural product perhaps, but they do not think of themselves as participants in agriculture. They think of themselves as "consumers". If they think beyond that, they recognise that they are passive consumers.'

Wendell Berry, Farmer[3]

---

3   Cited in Andrews, G (2008) *The Slow Food Story*, McGill-Queens University Press, p. 89

The problems of this consumer passivity are all around us. Our relationship with the food we buy and eat is no longer about straightforward nutrition. With increasingly tasty flavourings in our food products, our consumption of sugar and fat has increased, leading to a growing problem of obesity in the Western world. This loss of control has lead to occasions when decisions taken within the food industry have conflicted with the basic needs of its own consumers, in a series of scandals about the toxic nature of some food ingredients.

As these crises grew in number, consumers gradually awoke, as though from a bad dream. The disconnection between the producer and the consumer became obvious, and there were two main reactions. Firstly there was an extension of government regulation, then once-passive consumers become more motivated and engaged, more selective over the products that they bought.

Since these crises have happened quite regularly, consumers have become a little disillusioned over handing too much control to industrial agriculture. They have become more suspicious of the motivation of some food companies, believing that cosmetic appeal is often more valued than basic nutrition. Food purchasers have become less trusting, no longer leaving all the decisions to the corporates. In rejecting Fast, they have moved back towards selecting their own raw ingredients, and taking a greater interest in local food producers. Slow – spelt with a big 'S' – is all about authenticity over convenience.

The evolution of the food industry has distinct parallels with the financial sector. The two share some fundamental characteristics – relationships extending over longer distances, the growth in scale of the global, applied technologies which make it possible to develop and distribute products faster and the inclination towards greater complexity within processed products. This chapter explores the changes in behaviour of governments and consumers when the disconnection in the food sector has become most extreme. Given that the development of the food sector is somewhat ahead of the financial sector, the trends might offer some insight as to how the financial sector might evolve in the coming years.

Fast Food, Fast Finance

To understand our contemporary relationship with food, we need to take a step back into the 1950s; to walk into the Formica kitchen, and reach into the cupboard for a sachet of Tang. The orange-tasting powder, including vitamins A, C and artificial colouring, would be mixed with water to make a breakfast drink that symbolised everything that the post-war generation was looking for – convenience and modernity. In the same way that complex products like CDOs appeared to represent progress in finance decades later, reconstituted foods were at the cutting edge of innovation in the 1950s. Tang was the taste of progress.

'From the end of World War II until the 1970s, a lot of people honestly believed that the world was simply getting better and better, mostly because science and industry kept creating great new products and evermore convenient ways of living.'

Jane & Michael Stern[4]

The belief that agriculture and its products could be analysed, understood and perhaps changed for the better had a radical effect. In the field, farmers were promised 'Better living...through Chemistry',[5] as they were introduced to new products to manage soil fertility and agricultural pests. Food science led to processed products that were altered to enhance aspects of the eating experience, like taste or feel, or to solve issues such as the search for a longer shelf life or how to create perfectly uniform chips.[6] The focus was on making changes, and making the system more intensive: more efficient production, faster processing and wider distribution.

In finance, pushing the boundaries meant grappling with some very sticky problems about evaluating risk and return;[7] how to price products derived from other assets;[8] and how to anticipate the risk of loss on an investment in worst-case scenarios.[9] Some of the key features at the heart of these models were difficult to evaluate, but the models became associated with progress and were widely used. So widely used, in fact, that they helped speed up complex decision-making, enabling capital to move faster around the world. These models treated the

4   Cited in *Encyclopaedia of Pop Culture* (1992) Harper Perennial, pp. 505–507

5   DuPont Marketing Slogan, Source *DuPont: Heritage*

6   Schlosser, E (2001) *Fast Food Nation*, Penguin

7   Capital Asset Pricing Model, as cited in Fama, E.F. & French, K.R. (2004) *The Capital Asset Pricing Model:Theory and Evidence*

8   Black, F & Scholes, M (1973) *The Pricing of Options and Corporate Liabilities* The Journal of Political Economy, Vol. 81, No. 3. (May – Jun., 1973), pp. 637–654

9   Berry, R.P (2010) *Value at Risk: An overview of analytical VaR* JP Morgan Analytics & Consulting

economy like an engineering system, which could be broken into parts and analysed.[10] As the financial sector expanded, helped by the breakdown of old ideological divides between East and West, the models encouraged the perception that the risks within it were being measured, monitored and understood.

Scale and distance

As the cost of imported goods fell sharply from the 1980s onwards, consumers found that many food products were cheaper to import than grow and produce in the UK. Resources in less developed nations were easy to secure and came at a lower overhead cost. Imported food from Asia, South America and Africa replaced homegrown fare throughout the seasons. Small-scale farms were aggregated, and the local butcher-cum-abattoir could not compete. Globalisation swept in and the winds of change blew these once parochial production systems out of the marketplace. Advanced transport and refrigeration technologies even allowed foods grown overseas like fresh raspberries to be transported long distances from overseas, while economies of scale kept costs down. Now prawns consumed in the UK travel thirteen thousand miles to the table from Bangladesh.[11] The price paid for many exotic foodstuffs, produced via a network of long-distance food pathways, seems deceptively low.

By the 1990s, these long-distance pathways were under fire as environmentalists highlighted the wider impact of the 'world on a plate' culture. The issue led to the introduction of **Food Miles**,[12] a concept designed to highlight just how far food had travelled to the table. Food miles became a way to evaluate the origins of where food came from, and to promote the credentials of local produce. The concept has now been refined in the concept of **Fair Miles**,[13] and contributed to the proliferation of farmers' markets and urban vegetable plots that have recently transformed the food landscape into the post-modern era.

---

10 Banking Crisis: dealing with the failure of the UK banks Seventh Report of Session 2008–09 House of Commons

11 Sustain (1994) The Food Miles Report: *The dangers of long-distance food transport* (republished 2010, p. 11)

12 Introduced by the SAFE Alliance, now Sustain

13 Chi, K, MacGregor, J, King, R (2009) *Big Ideas in Development: Fair Miles*, IEED/Oxfam p. 9

Fig 2.2: Distance to the table

Apples – New Zealand
(14,000 miles)

Coffee – Brazil
(5,655 miles)

Avocado – Kenya
(4,237 miles)

 Wine – France
(461 miles)

 Tomato – Homegrown
(0 miles)

Copyright © 2011 Gervais Williams
Source: The Food Miles Report Sustain 2004, Gervais Williams

In the financial world, the economic distance between countries at different stages of development has brought opportunities. Relationships have extended over greater distances, initially driven by trade, but later by more speculative activity. The scale of this activity has mushroomed, and now far exceeds transactions carried out for commercial purposes. This has only heightened the gulf between investors and the providers of financial services. These gaps are at least as significant as in the food industry.

As investor interest has expanded to include global products, including organisations acting in different cultures and regulatory regimes, there has been action to acknowledge their responsibilities explicitly.[14] But there has

---

14 Socially Responsible Investing (SRI)

been less effort to address the geographical elements of investor behaviour *from the saver's perspective*. **Investment Miles**, introduced as a concept for the first time in this book, will do exactly that. The concept highlights the gap between the investor and the proximity and nature of their ultimate investment. Investment Miles is based on the premise that a closer link between the investor and the investment is a win-win situation. The investor can have the reassurance of reweighting their capital in an environment where returns are just as attractive, but where the risks are more known and transparent, with the potential positive spin-off benefits of stimulating the growth of the domestic economy, and creating employment locally. The full details of the concept of Investment Miles are included in Chapter 8.

Regulation: the limits to control

Pushing the boundaries in both the food and finance sectors has highlighted how little most people know about complex systems, particularly those with multiple feedback mechanisms. It has been known since the 1950s, for example, that some pesticides work synergistically in combination, amplifying adverse effects many times over. There are more than 350 pesticides approved and monitored in the UK, plus thousands of approved drugs. It is impossible to anticipate or test for every combination. Recent debate has focused on complex relationships between pesticide exposure and drugs for the treatment of stomach ulcers. In some cases, reactions can be extreme. We have to accept that there are limits. There are 'unknown unknowns'.

While some issues of this kind clearly arise from a lack of knowledge, the real trouble comes when the interests of producers and consumers diverge and are no longer aligned – in an imbalanced relationship. In the food industry, this occurred as long ago as the 1960s with the development of some sugar-coated cereals. They became the symbol of a failing system. By 1969, President Nixon's review of US food, nutrition and health prompted a debate worldwide on whether the food industry was developing poor quality foods. Some cereals were alleged to have less nutritional value than the packets in which they were sold. Senator Robert Choate, the campaigner that led the Nixon food review, believed these products had little to recommend them. '[T]hey fatten', he said 'but do little to prevent malnutrition.'[15] The outcome of the review gave the food regulator, the US

---

15 Cited in US *Time* magazine *Consumerism: Not by Cereal Alone* 17.08.70

Food and Drug Administration, more teeth, and led to voluntary guidelines on displaying nutritional details on food packaging.

Today, nutritional labelling is mandatory in both the US and the UK, but wrangling continues. Nixon believed that the industry would 'self-stabilise', but it frequently appears to have overstepped the mark. The problem lies in divergent motivations. Commercial food producers may maximise sales by interpreting regulatory boundaries in a legalistic manner, rather than in best helping consumers fully comprehend what it is that they are buying. Regulation tends to address problems retrospectively, and even then cannot anticipate all the outcomes. By drawing precise boundaries, regulation may encourage those with vested interests to look very closely at where lines are being drawn, and then optimise behaviour around those lines in the sand.[16] Indeed, there are armies of professional people that are trained and incentivised to do just that.

Repeated crises – related to the practices used in the intensive rearing of livestock, of cross-contamination in production, of innovation leading to harmful by-products – all highlight the challenges for regulators. Labelling is a minefield. Claims on foods have to be scientifically proven, but there are still ambiguities in the minds of consumers as to what terms like 'low fat', or 'light' mean. For the regulator, the aim is greater transparency from the industry, and better understanding for consumers. But what is delivered is not always crystal clear. In the process, it often appears that the consumer is not being well served. 'Is food labelling concerned with public health or just propaganda?' asked an article in the Journal of Medicine in 2010.[17] Perhaps investors in some of the new, leveraged financial products might be asking similar questions.

The history of finance is also marked by crises and waves of regulation. But prior to the crisis in 2008, the regulator's approach was 'light touch', based on the belief that the financial services industry would self-stabilise. It did not. In fact, seeking to optimise *around* the rules designed to make the financial system safer[18] is thought to have driven some of the innovation in the CDO market. Tranches of these products were 'labelled' AAA, but later it transpired that the assumptions about inter-relationships and the extent of default risk were incorrect. Deregulation allowed financial

---

16 See Kay, J (2010) *Obliquity*, Profile Books p85; cites Blastard & Dilmot's work on optimisation around a national target in the UK health service

17 Nestle, M, Ludwig, D.S *(2010) Front-of-Package Food Labels: Public Health or Propaganda?* Journal of the American Medical Association Volume 303 (8) pp. 771–772

18 Basel II

institutions to grow 'too big to fail'; we did not understand that banks would act as shock spreaders rather than shock absorbers. Within the industry, there is no striving for smallness because scale offers global advantages, and for those that provide high-street banking services there is the quasi-financial guarantee of the Government.

Time for change

Changing the mindset of a globalised industry that moves in the 'fast lane' may look unlikely. After all, compared with the food sector, the finance industry is more focused on narrow financial goals than other metrics. But with the setback of CDOs, there was a period when the confidence that dominated fields like risk management quickly ebbed away. If financial markets behaved as expected, the stock market crash of 1987, the turmoil in 1992 when the pound left the ERM and the 2008 crash would each be expected to take place around once in 12 billion years.[19]

The lesson from the food industry is that when crises pass through, there is a consequent long-term change in the mindset in the industry. The financial crisis of 2008 was much worse than those of previous decades. Everyone remembers the tangible fear of an imminent systemic collapse of financial institutions and banks around the world. Investors did exhibit a major change in behaviour at the time. But strangely that change of behaviour appears to have been transitory.

In contrast, following the BSE crisis, a large part of the UK population changed their eating habits. Initially most ceased to eat beef. Some ceased to eat meat altogether. In the following years, beef sales have recovered to a large degree. But even so there has been a major and long-term progression in the attitudes of consumers. In general they have become more informed about how their meat has been reared and are more discriminating in their purchases. Organic meat and high-integrity farm sales have subsequently grown to be a large part of the meat market. And food producers have amended their procedures to ensure that there is no risk of a similar crisis again.

But somehow, despite the gravity of the financial crisis in 2008, financial market participants have quickly reverted to their previous habits. Whilst CDOs are notably less popular, investor attitudes regarding complexity remain broadly unchanged. Investment banks are once again using sophisticated strategies to generate very large financial profits, and have

---

19 The Economist *A Special report on Financial Risk* 11.02.2010

resumed paying out telephone number bonuses. How has this come about? Why have professional investors not modified their behaviour in a more significant way? Why is it that private investors still remain largely passive over the kinds of assets allocated to their portfolios? How is it that the changes in the financial sector have been so slight when compared with those witnessed in the food sector?

Prior to 2008, the growth of the debt markets was largely created by the private sector. But following the 2008 financial crisis, the key source of credit has changed in an important way. Much of the liquidity that fuelled the recovery of financial markets up to 2011 has come from central banks and government. They were initially obliged to reflate their economies to offset the risks of systemic collapse of certain high street banks. Interest rates were brought down to record lows. Together, these actions rescued the financial sector. But by persisting with Quantitive Easing and super-low interest rates, the government has now restarted the credit expansion that otherwise would have ceased. So despite a brief interruption of service, the previous trajectory of the financial markets has not really changed despite the financial crisis of 2008. Consequently, the previous habits of market participants have become re-established. Professional investors have not really 'learnt' from the financial crisis in 2008, in the way that food consumers have 'learnt' from their various crises.

Habits are hard to change; bad habits most especially. The habits regarding the over-optimising of fast finance structures remain deep seated. The premise is that if global financial markets can withstand the shock of a crisis of the scale of 2008, then the trends of growing market liquidity are surely here to stay. This comfortable notion is a consequence of the responses taken by the authorities to mitigate the crisis. Cutting interest rates from 5.75 per cent to 0.5 per cent in the UK effectively rescued many highly-borrowed businesses and individuals through the sharp reduction in interest payments. Secondly, since most countries went into the crisis with government debt at modest levels, there has been ample scope for the authorities to provide emergency funding to the financial sector.

Subsequent to the crisis, governments have grown to rather like this strange financial balancing act. It offers some hope of an economic recovery that might boost tax take, and bring their budget outgoings and revenues more into balance. And there is a certain cosiness with government issuing bonds to finance its budget deficit and approving central banks to buy in the same bonds to boost the economy. So there is an uneasy financial truce that is the *status quo*.

This analysis highlights how heavily the trends of the financial markets are dependent upon the UK government's ability to persist with the current policies. But this equilibrium is not stable. A minor financial change in the current balance and the *status quo* ceases. The problems of the credit boom will then move back to centre stage. Excessive debt still overshadows the consumer sector, and some parts of the financial sector, but now the government sector is also over-borrowed.

The problem lies in the fact that when the next financial crisis comes, neither of the previous UK government strategies will be available. Interest rates cannot fall much further and the authorities do not have the same scope to take on further debt to re-liquify the financial sector. Meanwhile the financial markets continue to issue over-engineered products in spite of the fact that previous safety margins have been eroded. The next financial crisis will be one that cannot be resolved with quick fixes.

The need to slow

If the UK government, with all the power of legislation and the Bank of England behind it, cannot offer a solution to the problem, what chance do individual investors have when confronted by these challenges? One answer relates back to the previous comments from Wendell Berry. Individuals can become overwhelmingly powerful when they discriminate in a similar way together. If everyone stops purchasing certain products, this is disastrous for the relevant supplier.

Various organisations have sprung up to promote this agenda in the food industries. Many of these such as The Soil Association, Common Earth, and Compassion in World Farming have high degrees of integrity and have adopted the high moral ground. Although these organisations are not necessarily mutually cohesive, they often share common ideals, including a care for the environment and for human health. They are important because they energise consumers to recognise the risks of passive buying behaviour. At times of crisis in the food chain, their influence increases and they can lead large-scale change in consumer attitudes. These organisations champion the reconnection of producers and their customers. Typically they reject food products that are uniform, and champion raw food that embraces diversity. They celebrate food cultures that reflect the diverse characteristics of the local micro-climate and geology of each region. They seek to retain specific sub-species from past decades, and promote the seasonality of different fruits and vegetables.

Probably the most noteworthy food movement came into existence in Italy in 1986, as a result of an Agricola demonstration against the opening of a McDonalds fast-food restaurant. Agricola saw the 'Golden Arches' of the McDonalds' logo as a symbol of twentieth-century inflexibility. Among the protesters was Carlo Petrini, who then went on to found the Slow Food movement. Whilst the protest failed to stop the opening of a branch of McDonalds, it did lead to a manifesto promoting a shift away from the negative effects of fast food. It highlighted the consequences of serving uniform products irrespective of local variation. The movement sought to inform people about when, where and how their food was produced.

The supporters of the Slow Food movement anticipated and perhaps helped precipitate a widespread change in consumer attitudes and behaviour. They have highlighted many of the 'unknown unknowns' in industrial food production systems in general, and persuaded consumers to become more actively selective about their food purchases. Over the last twenty-five years, the market for fresh produce has changed to favour those products that are more naturally grown, including those that are grown organically. Whilst these products are more expensive, the consumer values the reduced unknowns associated with fewer biocides, pesticides or artificial hormones in the case of meat production. There has been a resurgence of interest in more wholesome ingredients, in 'growing your own', or buying directly from local farms. Farmers markets have sprung up all over the UK, and farm shops are growing in popularity. But the interest in Slow values has not stopped there. It now stretches far outside the food arena. Slow Travel has grown popular in the UK with the books of Alistair Sawday. Slow Parenting, Slow Fashion – the wider adoption of the movement reflects a growing interest in a deeper experience; a move away from the concentration on a series of narrow targets with all the consequent compromises that have to be made.

> 'We are addicted to speed, to cramming more and more into every minute. Every moment of the day feels like a race against the clock, a dash to a finish line that we never seem to reach. This roadrunner culture is taking a toll on everything... That is why the Slow Movement is taking off.'
>
> **Carl Honoré**, *In Praise of Slow*[20]

---

20 Honoré, C (2005) *In Praise of Slow: How a Worldwide Movement Is Challenging the Cult of Speed*, Orion Publishing

The Slow movement has a strong ethical bias. The agenda of the Slow movement, in all its various factions, promotes reconnecting consumers with the production of food ingredients, the pleasure of staying in smaller, more individual hotels, in taking time to make things with your children, in buying clothes that do not need to be changed when fashion changes. The Slow movement includes a renewed interest in rescaling, in the value of smallness, in minimising unnecessary consumption and waste, in making things more personal and thereby more relevant to the individual. This trend, very clear in 2011, was anticipated by the radical economist E.F. Schumacher back in the 1970s. 'As soon as great size has been created', he said, 'there is often a strenuous attempt to attain smallness within bigness.'[21]

What is striking is how far the ideas of Slow have entered the mainstream. Although there are Fast production systems all around us, it is the concepts of Slow that capture the *zeitgeist*. Whilst Slow attitudes are most developed in the food industry, many of the food industry's problems over issues of scale, of managing complex relationships, of grappling with issues consequent to distance, of relevance and connectedness – are all real in finance too.

Despite this, savers attitudes have been relatively passive regarding the activities within financial markets during the credit boom. Capital markets have been given a relatively free rein to transact with little constraint, and the asset price immediately subsequent to the transaction has been the principle metric of success. Fast finance has not been overly constrained by the sensibilities of those worrying about financial imbalances or risks to the national balance sheet. The main focus has been closing transactions to generate big profits, especially when followed by a quick sale of the investment on to others, so the capital is ready to be reused again for the next deal.

Slow Finance?

'Fast and Slow... are shorthand for ways of being, or philosophies of life. Fast is busy, controlling, aggressive, hurried, analytical, stressed, superficial, impatient, active, quantity-over-quality. Slow is the opposite: calm, careful, receptive, still, intuitive, unhurried, patient, reflective, quality-over-quantity...'[22]

Carl Honoré, *In Praise of Slow*

---

21 Schumacher, E.F (1973) *Small Is Beautiful: A Study of Economics as if People Mattered*, Penguin

22 Honoré, C (2005) *In Praise of Slow: How a Worldwide Movement Is Challenging the Cult of Speed*, Orion Publishing

Many would argue that the interests of investors cannot be reconciled with the principles of the Slow movement. Investors are almost wholly interested in just one factor, the return offered with respect to the risk. In contrast, the general principles of the Slow movement are not noted for their financial focus. It appears obvious that there is no overlap between these attitudes. They are mutually exclusive.

But these two positions are caricatures. They are given without context. The fact is that both groups represent values held within the range of opinions held by the wider community. So, for example, before a specific investment gains investor support, it must be convincing as to why it can be expected to deliver premium investment returns, and the attitude of those local to that investment may be highly relevant to the decision. Mining companies frequently find their investment plans disrupted because of concerns expressed by those living in the area, and because of the values of Government representing those concerns. What may appear to be a highly attractive investment opportunity in isolation can be worthless when set in context of the attitudes of the community local to it.

On top of this, the values and temperament of the wider community are not static. The lesson from the food sector is that sensibility can change, and change greatly at times of crisis. Fast finance has been in place for an extraordinarily long period. It has weathered the crisis of 2008. But it would be a mistake to assume that general values and beliefs towards the activities in the financial sector won't change. Quantitive Easing and super low interest rates may have deferred the debt hangover a bit longer. But the financial imbalances are continuing to grow. Either the policy of Government will change, or some financial shock overseas will unbalance the *status quo*.

The exact time and details of the next financial crisis cannot be predicted with precision. With the financial reserves of the authorities already depleted, the forthcoming setback will not be deferred again. Many sense this sea-change coming. There is a general feeling that the activities of the financial sector are in some ways unsustainable; that the interests of the wider public are being willfully compromised. But at present there isn't sufficient reason to articulate the uneasiness. Those outside the financial industry may be apprehensive over the risks of an oversized financial sector, but with the recovery of the markets they feel curiously disempowered.

So with the onset of the next financial crisis, the previous trends will come to an end. The great unwind of the debt mountain will start. Change will be here to stay. As with the food sector, there will be a profound change in opinion of the activities of the financial sector. The excesses of the previous trends will define the reaction. If expensive red sports cars have become associated with all that is negative about the financial boom, then expensive red sports cars will become extremely unpopular. By using this approach we can anticipate some of the consequent forthcoming changes in the public mood.

Fig 2.3: The principles of slow finance

Copyright © 2011 Gervais Williams

The huge growth in the use of debt has been a principle feature of the financial boom. Debt enhances return in rising markets, but increases the risk in falling markets. The reaction will be the **preference to be debt-free**. The sizable mortgages used to fund Buy-to-Let housing and second homes overseas can be expected to become incredibly unpopular for example.

Complex financial instruments have seen enormous growth during the last twenty-five years. The complexity of CDOs has already cost investors. The straightforward reaction will be that simplicity will be favoured, whilst complexity will be rejected. Investors will refocus capital to those **investments that are simple and easy to comprehend**.

During the credit boom, rapid growth has become equated with rapid return. There has been a growing willingness to pay up for growth – growth companies, growth markets. But expectations of rapid growth may be the area of greatest setback after the crisis. The new attitude will equate rapid growth with greater uncertainty and risk. So in future investors may be more inclined to support businesses with more **careful and sustained expansion plans**.

With the credit boom, there has been an obsession with bigness, large transactions, investment portfolios limited to the largest stocks. But the debt hangover can be expected to constrain the world growth on which larger companies depend. The reaction to this trend could be **a renewed interest in smallness,** investing in all companies that have scope to expand in the absence of world growth.

Over the last twenty-five years the financial sector has grown increasingly disconnected from the local economy. There may be hostility to trading strategies that take no responsibility for the consequent risks to the national balance sheets. There will be a real risk that adverse Government fiat may levy windfall taxes on those investment strategies that overlook the wider risks. The new attitudes will insist on a reconnection with the underlying purpose of investing. **Investment strategies with demonstrable benefits for the national community will be favoured.**

The investment trends of the last twenty-five years have favoured those chasing hot themes for capital gain, whilst largely ignoring dividends. Markets could languish for a long period in future suggesting that the net gains from chasing hot themes might be zero. It will be recognised that better, more sustainable returns can be made by **compounding strategies based upon good and growing dividends**.

In rapidly rising markets many fund managers have relied on stock market indices to keep up with the market. Most regular portfolios are dominated by big cap index holdings, even those the fund managers believe are unattractive investments, because a zero weighting could lead to the underperformance of the rising Index. The new attitude will favour portfolios with a sole focus on those stocks with improving prospects in absolute terms, **selecting only those selected companies that the investment manager is truly keen to support**.

These new values and beliefs are defined by reacting to the current trends that have become overextended and ultimately costly to the clients. These are some of the most obvious examples, but each individual will have a slightly different view on the trends that they find most unattractive. Opinions may differ, but the general trend will be an unstoppable shift in public values as a reaction to the excesses.

A new investment strategy for the coming period can be assembled from the principles highlighted above, specifically limiting the investment pool to those selected companies that the investment manager is really keen to support. The preferred investments will be those that are simple and easy to comprehend, largely debt-free, offering careful and sustained expansion plans and demonstrable benefits for the national community, with investors adopting a renewed interest in smallness and a compounding strategy based upon good and growing dividends.

What is striking about this strategy is how closely it matches that of the agenda of the established Slow movement. The next crisis can be expected to shift the financial values and beliefs of much of the wider community closer to those of the Slow movement, in a similar way to that seen within much of the food industry. This should not be a surprise since the problems of globalisation in the food industry have been widely replicated in the financial sector. The new investment strategy has the real advantage of delivering value, both to the investor and the national community, after the current trends come to an end. Its ethics will reflect those of the wider public too.

Socially Responsible Investment

Some might question how the Slow Finance strategy differs from that already promoted by Government, that of Socially Responsible Investment (SRI). Empiricism is the key differential. In its title, SRI seeks to reweight investment decisions a little more in favour of the interests of the wider community outside of the financial markets. But although SRI shares the same ideals as that of Slow Finance, its agenda has been defined during a time of financial optimism. It may be a reaction to the financial sector during the credit boom, but at this stage the wider community doesn't know where the worst excesses will be found.

SRI's problem is promoting the wider social agenda in the absence of general engagement from the public. There may be excellent arguments as to why it should be pursued, but these are mainly intellectual. In the absence of an emotional drive, it doesn't get a lot of buy-in from the decision makers in the financial world. SRI is normally implemented by Code, with lists of what is theoretically believed to be in the interests of investors and the wider communities as agreed by august bodies. It forces the agenda on many of those who do not fully appreciate the reasoning. During the period of the credit boom the SRI factors seem to offer little prospect for outperformance.

Since SRI is not seen as central to the process of adding value in stock selection, fund management organisations have recruited SRI teams or departments that determine how well individual businesses comply with the desired goals. Others outsource this requirement to specialist SRI organisations. The point is that SRI is implemented as a process that is secondary to the investment decision. SRI is not truly integrated within the investment process.

In contrast, following the change in general financial values, the Slow Finance agenda will be defined by those areas that have cost investors. It will have widespread emotional backing from the investment managers as well as the wider public. Slow Finance will be adopted because the factors it highlights are seen as improving the risk/reward ratio of the investment decision.

CDOs lead to large financial losses during the financial crisis of 2008. Whilst the SRI agenda does seek to avoid the problems of excessive complexity, the codes overlooked the risks inherent in the CDO structure. And even those individuals that spotted the risk in CDOs were remote from the investment process.

The Slow Finance agenda is empirically based, with its agenda set by those areas of the worst excesses. So Slow Finance will be much more integral to investment decision-making than SRI. Indeed it may be that it is so integral that SRI staff can be fused into the fund management operations in future. The ethical issues will be addressed in the investment meetings between the fund manager and the management of the company seeking investment capital. Checklists may be used in this process, but they will not be strictly necessary, since nearly everybody will be on a similar agenda.

Moving one step ahead

Financial markets differ from food markets in one very significant way. Food is consumed, so new food buying decisions need to be made almost every day. In contrast, equity investments are semi-permanent. Savers have no need to make investment decisions every day or indeed on any specific timeframe. Once they have invested, they can sit back and wait. Although there are new companies floated on the stock market, and some that get taken over or go into liquidation, investors can only buy a finite amount of stock in the most attractive companies. Those that invest ahead of others in the companies that become most desirable are disproportionately rewarded. Early adopters that correctly anticipate the market trends are boosted by other investors chasing the bandwagon, and paying higher prices for the limited pool of investments held by the first movers.

There is therefore real value in gaining a good understanding of the Slow principles before the coming change of investor temperament. Slow investments are likely to outperform at the time of the next crisis and beyond, in spite of the stock market itself being highly volatile at that time. It will be difficult to finesse the best entry point, since it is likely there will be great uncertainty at that time. However there is advantage in being prepared ahead of a change of trend in what are regarded to be the best investments.

The next chapters will focus upon how it is possible to identify opportunities even in more difficult economic times. There is robust evidence that factors highlighted by *Slow Finance* have, in fact, been delivering premium returns that have been largely overlooked during the period of the credit boom. It is time to go Slow.

3

SLOW IN PRACTICE: STOCK MARKET RISKS AND OPPORTUNITIES

'We under-estimate the effect of randomness in about everything.'
Nassim N Taleb, *Fooled By Randomness*[1]

Chance has a big impact on what happens in our lives. However we don't really recognise this. We often link recent events together in our mind in a narrative of cause and effect, though the events themselves are often unrelated. Nassim Taleb describes this as 'narrative fallacy'.[2] We hear it all the time on the news, particularly with regard to the explanations for the movements of the stock market. There are almost always at least two equally convincing reasons available to justify either the rise or the fall. The news editor just chooses the appropriate one depending upon the direction of the market's move.

It is a bit like that with our memories. We are most effective at remembering things where we predicted correctly, and forget lots of other things when the outcome was not as expected. Our recollection is not quite as accurate as we like to think.[3] This is something of a handicap in the financial world, since overconfidence in predicting the specific events can lead to costly investment mistakes. On top of this, a large number of events are precipitated by things that are both unknown and unknowable.[4] Chance plays a much greater part in the ultimate movement of share prices and stock markets than most investors appreciate.

---

1   Taleb, N. N (2008) *Fooled By Randomness: The Hidden Role of Chance in Life and in the Markets*, Random House

2   Taleb, N. N (2007) *The Black Swan: The Impact of the Highly Improbable*, Random House

3   Zeckhauser, R (2010) *The Known, the Unknown, and the Unknowable in Financial Risk Management: Measurement and Theory Advancing Practice*, eds Diebold, Francis, Doherty, N & Herring, H, Princeton University Press

4   Zeckhauser, R (2010) *The Known, the Unknown, and the Unknowable in Financial Risk Management: Measurement and Theory Advancing Practice*, eds Diebold, Francis, Doherty, N & Herring, H, Princeton University Press

So, even before thinking about the best positioning of our savings, there are real advantages in pinning down all those factors we *do* have in our control. For example, do we understand what investment outcome represents a success? To help clarify this, we can use an analogy with three individual roulette gamers.

The first roulette player knows the rules of the roulette table, but he has little interest or patience in reading theories of probability or gaming strategies. He is at the casino for excitement. He knows that he could lose everything that he owns, so he only brought with him what he can afford to lose. Apart from this bit of self-preservation, he has no coherent betting strategy, and simply looks to respond to the trends on the night. If he feels lucky, he will bet large. If unsure, he'll bet small. It is probably the most erratic way to gamble, relying on pure instinct, but for many, it is the most thrilling.

The second gambler has a different strategy. He too knows that the odds are strongly in favour of the casino and that, in the long-term, the house will always grind the player down. The house has the edge and it is almost impossible to come up with a strategy that will guarantee a win. He understands risk and looks to take some decent winnings if chance favours him. And so he plays a steady game, making a steady bet of one chip for every spin of the wheel. He knows that most of the time the wheel will go against him, but by placing a single, small bet on a number every time, sometime it will come up. If it comes up early, he makes a great gain and leaves the table a winner. If not, at least he can sit back, dreaming of the potential big win each spin, and enjoy the hospitality that the casino provides. At least he gets fed, even if he does lose his complete stake.

A third man comes to the table. Unlike the laid back attitude of our second man or the flamboyance of the first, he concentrates hard. He is equipped with a pen and paper, and he notes down the sequence of numbers that have just come up on the roulette wheel. He is looking for any advantage he can find. Perhaps the wheel is uneven. He tries to charm the croupier, believing a happy croupier is a croupier who may be on his side. This is a man who will do anything to minimise his risk of loss. If he really knew the field, he might admit that it is all pointless. But there is always a chance something has been missed, and he enjoys looking for it.

So the croupier spins. The three gamblers have their bets on the table and their numbers chosen. They all want to enjoy the rush of a profitable win, but each has a different approach to managing chance. They each have different expectations and different risk tolerances as to how they plan to get to their desired outcome. But, most importantly, they plan ahead *in their own degree* so that if luck goes against them they are not surprised. And if the luck is with any one of them, they leave the casino a winner.

Of course, investing in stock market businesses is not a game of roulette. The long-term trend is that the stock market rises over time,[5] so this 'roulette wheel' is firmly in the investors' favour. There are risks of course, and investors can lose all of their capital, although this is unusual.

If the three roulette gamers were to try their luck at investing, what kinds of investors would they be? The first gambler is a pure **Speculator**. He has little regard for financial fundamentals or detailed analyst reports. He watches the market trends and when the trend is with him he bets big. He invests aggressively in the hope that the right call will give him a fast and lucrative pay-off. He knows that getting the timing right with a large bet-size will make him a tidy profit.

The second gambler has more regard for the unpredictability of the stock market and a greater appreciation of risk. To counter both, he plays a long game. He invests because stock markets tend to go up, but he plays a low-risk, low involvement game. He is a **Passive Investor**.

The third fellow is an **Active Investor**. He is interested in finding the best investments and hopes to take advantage of market opportunities. He knows that the harder he works, the bigger odds will be in his favour. He is still very open to a large fluctuation of returns, but at least his decisions focus on areas where chance favours him.

So, there we have it. There are three types of investors: the momentum Speculator; the low-risk Passive Investor; and the fine-tuned Active Investor. For those who have read up on investment strategies from the past, this trio may be ringing bells. These are the three types of investor identified in one of the most important texts written on investor behaviour, *The Intelligent Investor*[6] by Benjamin Graham. A classic text, first published more than fifty years ago, it is still relevant on the subject of serious investing.

Risky business

Benjamin Graham was one of the first investment strategists to recognise how much the movement of share prices influences how investors feel, and

---

5   See Dimson, E, Marsh, P, Stauton, M (2011) *Credit Suisse Global Investment Returns Yearbook* p. 12
    London Business School, for real ie inflation-adjusted equity returns around the world 1900–2010

6   Graham, B (1986) *The Intelligent Investor* 4th edition, Harper & Row

how that, in turn, has an effect on the investment decisions they consequently make. Financial risk does not just lie where most of us look for it – in the economy or in our investment portfolio – but it is also engrained within ourselves and our characters. Understanding this is vital.

Graham was wary of speculation. He believed speculators often confused themselves with investors. The difference is straightforward: an investor looks at a stock market share as part of a business, through the eyes of an owner. The speculator views himself as gambling with share prices of uncertain intrinsic value. For the speculator, value is only determined by what someone else will pay for the asset. Share price is all important. Graham recognised that a good speculator can still make a good return, but it is a different skill to investing. To paraphrase Graham: there is intelligent speculating as well as intelligent investing. Just be sure you understand which one is being practiced.

It is the fact that our decision-making can be so heavily affected by the movement of share prices that causes the problem. For most, the aim is to time their purchases to catch an upwave in the share price. Whilst the individual may consider himself as an investor, Graham said this was the action of a speculator. Since the share price was the motivation for the purchase, the problem comes when the share price trend reverses. This individual is largely disconnected from the fair value of their asset. When the share price peaks out they freeze and hope it goes up again and when the loss becomes too large they capitulate and sell the investment to ease the pain. As financial expert Graham Hooper[7] from MAM funds says: 'Too many investors find themselves on the black ski run, when really they would have much preferred the blue.' To take the analogy further, there is no point in going down the black run if you have not planned ahead to take advantage of the jumps and steep corners. Benjamin Graham passionately believed that investors needed to recognise the volatility of the stock market before they did anything else. Once this was recognised, at least they could plan ahead to make this volatility work for them.

How markets work: meet Mr. Market

The Intelligent Investor introduces a very helpful personification of the way the stock market operates. *Mr. Market* is a metaphorical business partner who comes to have a 'conversation' with the investor each day. He arrives

---

7   Graham Hooper, Distribution Director, MAM Funds

at the stockholder's door, offering to buy or sell his shares at a different price each day. *Mr. Market* can be erratic, swinging from euphoria to gloom in an instant. The price *Mr. Market* quotes often may seem plausible but; on other occasions it will be ridiculous. The investor is free to either agree with *Mr. Market*'s quoted price and trade with him, or ignore him. Graham believed that the intelligent investor should not regard the whims of *Mr. Market* as truly determining the value of the shares. That meant that the investor should try to profit from market folly, rather than become a victim of it. The investor is best off concentrating on the underlying performance of his companies and receiving dividends, not reacting to *Mr. Market's* irrational daily behaviour.

Mr. Market can be summed in three basic character traits:

1. **Regularity.** *Mr. Market* offers a market price for each stock every day.
2. **Irrationality.** The price offered may seem bizarre, and may not necessarily reflect long-term market trends or fair value.
3. **Moodiness.** *Mr. Market*'s prices fluctuate between incredible optimism and overwhelming depression. It all depends on how he is feeling on the day.

Even before I read *The Intelligent Investor*, I had used a similar metaphor for the equity market. Benjamin Graham had a title for his 'character' so I have come up with a name for my own, reflecting some of the additional characteristics I ascribe to the stock market today. *Ms. Market* is extraordinary.

Introducing *Ms. Market*

Graham's *Mr. Market* is a complex character. With the ability to swing from exuberant over-confidence to the depths of despair, *Mr. Market* shows elements of manic-depressive behaviour. My personification of the equity market, *Ms. Market* is mercurial too. She also has a dark side, but her mood swings are more calculating and can be even more severe. *Ms. Market* reassures to bolster confidence, then, just when you think you are ahead, she disappoints you. Yet when the market is low, she finds ways to stop you picking up bargains. If you find one, she drops the price to see if she can shake you out. *Ms. Market* goes out of her way to be difficult.

Ms. Market also comes and offers to transact every day. Not once, but many times. She is dangerous. By making trends obvious, and offering to trade all the time, she gives the impression that investing is not dangerous at all. The door is always open. She will encourage you to commit during times of market momentum, then gives you reasons to hold on when the markets turn. She enjoys your capitulation at the market bottom, leaving you carrying sizable losses.

When managing *Ms. Market*, the first step is to know what you are dealing with. *Ms. Market* is a threat, so keep your head. You need to know when an investment is cheap, really cheap, and make sure you recognise when it is a good time to buy. The Slow Investor wants to select investments when there is a great chance of making an attractive return, not follow those made when they are overwhelmed by the excitement of everyone getting in together. And occasionally, just occasionally, the Slow Investor would like to make an absolute bundle. I tend to call this kind of perfect investment opportunity a 'peach'.

Peaches, in the investment sense, do not come along very often, but the Slow Investor should always be on the lookout for them. Peaches are hard to find. They do not appear in the usual places, like stockbroker's reports or in the financial press. They are hidden away in the dusty corners of failed investments. Peaches also have lots of uncertainty surrounding them. They are difficult to analyse because there is usually little third party information available. But like any good investment sleuth, the Slow Investor should be able to follow the clues towards the logical conclusion.

It is best to search alone for peaches although this makes finding them hard work. To spot the Peach of an Investment, the Slow Investor will need to look into those areas that *Ms. Market* keeps out of sight. Look in those regions where no one else will be looking. Be happy to review investments where your colleagues will think you are wasting your time. But, be warned: If *Ms. Market* spots investors searching in a promising area, she will immediately try to divert your attention. She will raise prices of the oversold stocks to make them appear too expensive to be worth further investigation, and shift your attention towards something more conventional.

So, when you go looking for a Peach of an Investment, go alone, and keep the good news quiet when you find it.

Finding a Peach of an Investment

For those who are interested in identifying a Peach of an Investment – and who would not be? – there are seven key characteristics which define those who have a degree of success in finding them.

Fig 3.1: Finding peaches

Be Patient

Bide your time whilst waiting for that great investment opportunity to come along. Know that it might be a long wait. No matter. Be patient while nature runs its course. In time, you will come across an opportunity when you least expect it – possibly even two or three. But beware, if you feel you are overdue a Peach, you may be tempted to seize an under-ripe opportunity.

Be Open-minded

Frequently Peaches are found in sectors where others have not looked, or where they have looked but failed to see the facts. To spot a Peach, Slow Investors need to have an open-mind. They need to be willing to weigh the fundamentals without prejudice. This is even harder when the investor has come across a similar situation before, and most particularly in those cases when the investor has made unsuccessful decisions in similar situations in the past.

Have Self-belief

To harvest a Peach, you need the ability to make your own decisions. This is hardest when the investment crowd is doing something different. As social animals, our actions are very heavily influenced by the crowd, by how our actions will be judged by others. This makes it more difficult to make our own decisions when they look counter-intuitive. When selecting investments that appear counter-intuitive, believe in yourself.

Keep Emotions in Check

Recognise how your emotions influence the rational decision-making process. Being as dispassionate as possible helps you to spot the Peaches. Never let *Ms. Market* dictate your emotions. Instead, recognise how your emotions might conflict with your own estimates of a business's value, based on a straightforward and rational examination of the facts.

Gain Foresight

Most people's first investment is made at a time when the stock market momentum is strong. At times like this, nearly everyone thinks they have a good chance of being a successful investor. Once reassured, you are tempted to invest in a slightly larger size. And then, without explanation, the positive trend comes to end. Your investment falls sharply in price and your conviction disappears. Don't let the market determine when you choose to invest.

Cultivate Discipline

Be disciplined in your approach, and be sure that you do not allow the wrong mental linkages to cloud your judgment. In some cases, not transacting will be the most lucrative move you can make.

Back Your Confidence in Scale

Knowing what a Peach looks like is the first step. When you find a Peach, the next step is to trust your judgment. Do not be put off if you mention it to others, as they are likely to exhibit surprise. If you really do find a Peach, then it is important to back your judgment in sufficient scale.

These points, lightly made, are underpinned by some very serious messages: Investing can be risky; failing to understand and manage the risks will have a price – both real and psychological.[8] The latter is not a straightforward proposition. On the stock market, events move at pace. Investors are inundated with information.[9] Investors suffer from recollection bias, which distorts how they perceive past events and assess the prospect of them happening again,[10] and we tend to trust our own information more

---

8   Standard risk warnings highlight that past performance is not a guide to future performance

9   Information overload. See Dreman, D (1998) *Contrarian Investment Strategies: Going against the Crowd*, Simon & Schuster

10 Zeckhauser. R (2010) *The Known, the Unknown, and the Unknowable in Financial Risk Management: Measurement and Theory Advancing Practice*, eds Diebold, Francis, Doherty, N. & Herring, H, Princeton University Press, p. 89

than that supplied by anyone else[11]. Faster capital flows mean faster reversals, bringing potential for larger gains and more significant losses, both of which can trigger real physical responses.[12] And, of course, some of these trends are exacerbated by automated trading. It is no surprise, then, that even professional money managers feel pressure at times, and have been observed showing emotional mood swings.[13] How we manage these tensions is very important indeed.

So, as an investor, take a Slower approach. Understand yourself and prepare to explore your own investment strategy. Before doing that, perhaps there is time for a narrative to illustrate the many challenges in the search for premium returns.

Seeking the Next Microsoft

It is early June 1989. The memories of the 1987 stock market crash and many of the doom-laden press headlines that followed it have been viewed as overly negative. You, and a friend who works for a stockbroker, meet up for a meal.

Charles is clever. He talks about how exciting the stock market is after the Big Bang deregulation, and his infectious energy makes you feel quite upbeat. News of the recent election success of Solidarity in Poland gives you an even better feeling about the future. And you have been working hard and saving hard. Charles works in investments and perhaps it's time for you to think seriously about investing some of that capital. The conversation turns to picking a good stock market investment for the long term. No speculative short-term strategy. You want to find it, invest your capital and forget about it for a long time. It is a fairly passive strategy, since you just do not have the time or inclination to follow the markets every day.

Charles tells you about his recent successes. Microsoft Inc, a programme writer for IBM Portable Computers, has developed something called a Digital Operating System – DOS. It's been on the stock market for the last three years and the share price has already risen by over two and half times its original value. Or there is a little-known company called Apple (remember, it is 1989!). Apple makes computers that are different. The company is also

---

11 Zeckhauser. R (2010) *The Known, the Unknown, and the Unknowable in Financial Risk Management: Measurement and Theory Advancing Practice*, eds Diebold, Francis, Doherty, N. & Herring, H, Princeton University Press, p. 96

12 Zweig, J (2010) *Fear* Behavioral Finance and Investment Management (December 2010): 24–46

13 LeBaron, D (1974) *A Psychological Profile of the Portfolio Manager: Have recent upheavals made the portfolio manager manic depressive, a game player, or too much the organization man?* Reprinted in the Journal Of Behavioural Finance & Investment Management (2010) December, pp. 118–124

doing well, and its stock price is also two and half times its 1985 value. Which one to chose? They are both 'hot' stocks. You're uncertain. Isn't there a company based in the UK that you can invest in? Something that could also turn into a 'hot' stock and make a distinctly British, but decent investment.

Charles thinks not. The UK is not a place where stocks as hot as IBM, Microsoft and Apple reside. In fact, Charles' last new issue was a small business from Yorkshire, which paints and assembles steel frameworks for high-rise buildings. So you have two stock options: Microsoft or Apple. But who to choose? Charles points out that you aren't a serious investor, so why not decide with a toss of a coin. The coin gets flipped and you win. Charles owes you some shares in Microsoft.

Three years later, the UK has weathered a recession and it has been a tough time for the UK stock market. But you have prospered. Events in Poland ultimately led to the Berlin Wall being torn down and the reuniting of Germany. It has been all change with the pound leaving the ERM, but now UK interest rates are back at more sensible levels. Perhaps it is time to review your investment. You call Charles and arrange to meet for a drink. He arrives in a new suit, just back from a three-week holiday in the Caribbean. Clearly trading is treating him well. And how is the market treating your investment? Well, you are investing for the long term, so you never expected to get rich quick, but it would be nice to see some early return. Charles produces stock charts for both Microsoft and Apple.

Apple is not doing so well. Businesses chose to buy IBM clones rather than the proprietary computers from Apple. So Microsoft is up six times what Charles paid for them on your behalf. And Apple? Apple shares are up, but only up by 40 per cent. Still a good return compared to the average UK companies you could have invested in. You ask Charles about the company he bought to the market in May 1989. 'Oh that one', says Charles. 'They've had it really tough. Demand for new steel buildings has fallen back and it's loss making. The share price has collapsed by 80 per cent from the time of the issue.' You laugh, with a feeling of relief. It is lucky you have a good stock picker for a friend. Investing in Microsoft was certainly a peachy move.

Charles has some more advice. 'You could have bought either Apple or Microsoft. It all hinged on the flip of a coin. You bought Microsoft and it's up so much already that you have a capital gains tax liability.' However, take note. Trying to pick a stock like Apple or Microsoft before they explode upwards is as difficult as picking a needle out of a haystack. You rarely hear from people who invest in turkeys, for the simple reason nobody wants to tell others about their failures.

So what would have happened to your investment in the end? Would you have continued on a winning streak or overseen another investment failure? Apple became the largest company in the world. From the end of 1992, to the end of 2010, the stock appreciated by twenty-one times its 1989 value. Microsoft has also done well. Its growth rate slowed after the 1990s, but it started paying dividends which you chose to reinvest. Since you bought in June 1989, it has appreciated by seventy-four times, or with income reinvested, by ninety-three times. That is a staggering return, and one that sounds terribly impressive to anyone who is interested in stocks and shares. *Remember – it is the exception, not the rule.*

Come the end of 2010, whatever happened to the little steelwork business in the UK? The company has had a terrific period of growth over the last twenty years. It grew to become the largest steel erection business in the UK. Recently it agreed to set up a subsidiary in India where it has a chance of replicating its success. Since the end of 1992, the company's share price has risen by forty-nine times its original value. Given that they have paid out more generous dividends than Microsoft, had you reinvested these then your total gain would have been one-hundred-and-six times your investment by the end of 2010. Perhaps Charles should have taken your advice back in that restaurant in 1989!

This is a very simplistic story. But it is useful to use as an illustration of how investors fit in to the three broad investor types defined by Graham – the Speculator, the Passive Investor and the Active Investor. There are many individuals whose principle aim is to buy shares (or funds) that are rising fast, and that go on to hit further highs in the months after they have been purchased. These would be classified as Speculators according to Graham. Despite assumptions to the contrary, Graham believed that speculation was part of a healthy marketplace. He felt that speculative behaviour often helped companies to raise finance, especially those growing rapidly. He also believed that speculation funded innovative investment in businesses where cashflow might be negative for some time, through the prospect of capital gains; companies such as those with a good chance of announcing a transforming event such as a series of successful oil wells, or the development of novel medical treatments.

Graham defined these investors as Speculators because their principle return comes from the appreciation of the share price of their investment.

Their investment behaviour is highly attuned to buying early and enjoying a long rise of the share price. But in current parlance this group is now known as Growth Investors. Both Microsoft and Apple are good examples of the kinds of companies Growth Investors might find attractive. They had the prospect to grow at a very fast pace for many years.

One of the fastest rising Growth investments in the UK was Punch Group plc, the pub company. During the credit boom, its share price went from around £2 to over £13 in the five years between 2002 and 2007; a startling rise that took it into the FTSE100 Index. Shareholders who had invested since 2003 ended up with substantial notional profit of 450 per cent, and dividends added a further 30 per cent on top of that. However, between the middle of 2007 and March 2009, the Punch share price fell back from £13 to under 40p, because the company was heavily indebted in the credit crunch. So the investor who held for the entire period actually recorded a capital loss after seven years that exceeded the dividend income they had received in the period.

Growth investors know that they make a good annual return as long as the share price continues to rise. But when the share price starts to trend down, Speculators are vulnerable. Since most of their return is rolled up in the share price rise, they stand to lose all of their return quite rapidly if they do not crystalise the gain by selling the shares after the price has peaked. Growth investors tend to be very sensitive to a change in share price trend. Once they are convinced the share price has peaked, they do not wait around to see how low the share price may fall. Growth investors have a natural tendency to sell falling shares.

Other investors have an alternative strategy of buying shares that are unpopular, and often drifting lower in spite of a rising stock market. These investors are what Graham called Active Investors. In the modern context, many Growth Investors would consider themselves to be active, so bottom-fishing participants are known as Value Investors. Investments out of fashion tend to those that are stagnant or suffering declines in profits. But depressed investments can be perfect investments for Value Investors; when the decline is arrested, they return to growth and become more popular, driving up their share prices. But this may not happen, so Value Investors assume that a large part of their return will come from dividend distributions from the company or from takeovers from other competitors buying them. In contrast to the Growth Investor, the Value Investor is not unhappy with a share price that is falling. Providing the underlying business continues to generate good levels of cash, the Value Investor is often keen to buy more shares if the share price drifts lower.

Graham's Passive Investors do not fit readily into either group. It is true that many Passive Investors put their savings into Index funds which are made up of both those shares moving to new daily highs, and also those that are moving to new daily lows. But in modern times most of these investors prefer actively managed funds,[14] albeit with a substantial component of holdings within the benchmark index. Over the period of the credit boom, these types of funds have become popular given that they have kept up with the rapid rise of the overall market. Rather than call them Passive Investors, it is more appropriate to call these investors Index Plus Investors or Index Investors for short.

Despite the narrative above, there are very few well-known companies that produce outstanding returns over the long-term. Microsoft and Apple are two in a very short list. While Microsoft and Apple may have looked like Peach Investments in terms of return, in my mind they were not. They are well known stock exchange winners, selected for the story with the benefit of hindsight. But with returns like that, it is easy to see why they might have been confused with being a Peach. Most high growth companies disappoint within a few years. Back in 1989 it would have been near impossible to be sure these growth companies would succeed when most others did not. Even from 1992 it would have been difficult to identify that Apple and Microsoft had a good chance of going up as much as they did compared with most other growth investments.

But did you spot the real Peach? It was, in fact, a company called Severfield-Rowan plc (previously Severfield-Reeve plc before 1998). It was small when it floated in May 1989, and with the UK recession its share price fell back and it became a very tiny quoted company. However, as an investment, it was full of potential. *Ms. Market* hid it, highlighting lots of interesting Growth investments instead. Hardly anyone was watching Severfield-Rowan, with the share price dropping out of view.

But for those who were alert, Severfield-Reeve was a Peach of an opportunity to make a very substantial return. This company delivered a one hundred fold return, and yet the overall scale of the company still did not become large enough to register as one of the largest quoted companies

---

14 Actively managed: Funds managed by a professional, whose investment activities may diverge from those represented by a benchmark within a particular investment universe

in the UK, let alone the US! Truly *Ms. Market* keeps the Peach investments well hidden. Even when they pay out in huge size, most investors never even notice them. And although the capital gain on Severfield-Rowan was very large over the period between 1993 and the end of 2010, it is noteworthy that more than half of the return came from good and growing dividend income.

It would be incorrect to suggest that there are hundreds of Severfield-Rowans in the stock market, but there are quite a good number of stocks that deliver highly attractive returns, even in a slow growth world constrained by debt. The good news, if there is any good news, is that during the credit boom many more investors have become inclined to prefer growth investing when compared to value investing. For this reason when there are market setbacks, there are relatively fewer investors searching for value investments than might be anticipated. Peach investments will never be entirely obvious as *Ms. Market* keeps them well hidden. Even in the UK, there are over two thousand quoted companies, and worldwide there are over twenty-five thousand.[15] But with the advantage of knowing the Slow principles, and with the right mental attitude, some of the best investments can be found. Slow Finance aims to narrow the pool of potential investments to much improve the chances of finding Peaches. But before we address that issue, it is important that all investors note Graham's strategy that profits from the volatility of the stock market. Only by being well prepared for the rainy days can investors have sufficient capital to back their judgments when the opportunities become most attractive.

---

15   Source: Heriot-Watt University, Scotland

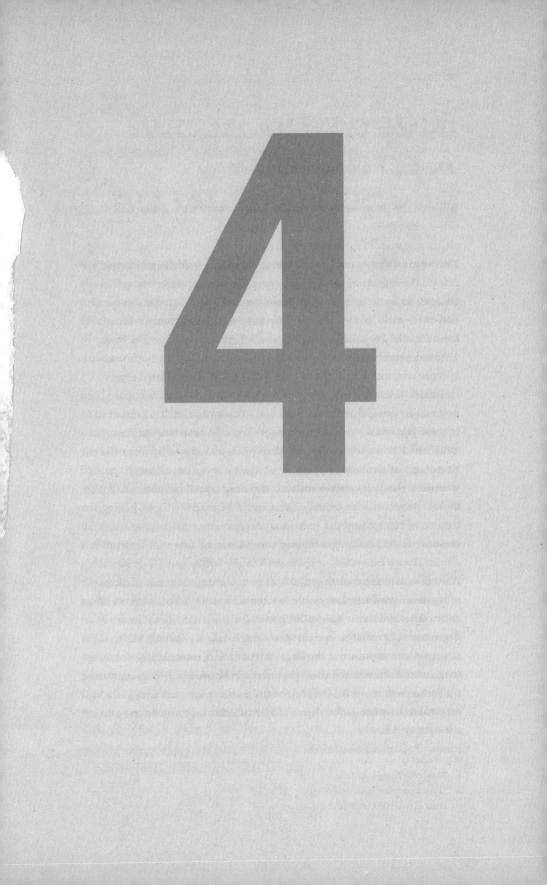

INVESTING SLOW: A STRATEGY FAVOURING VALUE

The seventeen years prior to the year 2000 were a 'golden age', as assets in many different markets rose year after year. Borrowing became progressively cheaper, so structures involving debt become more popular. Those who borrowed early made out like bandits, with asset prices rising very substantially. For example, many who bought the average UK house in 1985 enjoyed a five-fold rise up to 2007;[1] those who bought the house with a 90 per cent mortgage enjoyed a fifty-fold rise in their investment.

Get rich fast strategies, designed to make quick capital gains, have been particularly popular in this period. Since Benjamin Graham's time (up to the 1970s), several new categories of financial instruments have been established. Stock market indices, derivatives and spread betting offer the advantage of dealing in clusters of assets together; through geared[2] structures they offer the potential to make big capital gains on small price moves. Better still for many, profits could be made without having the trouble of researching the individual companies or assets that made up the instrument. Although trading these kinds of financial instruments almost always generated a capital gain in the 1980s and the 1990s, since 2000 the pattern has changed to a degree. During the stock market sell-offs[3], these products exaggerate on the downside. Now many of these derivitative products have a stop-loss feature that clicks in with an automatic sale after a certain percentage fall. By selling early, these strategies aim to miss out the larger part of the market falls, so that once the market has bottomed these products can be used heavily again during the subsequent recovery. The scale of the market recoveries after 2003, and even more so since 2009, then offered substantial gains once again on these strategies.

---

1   Nationwide House Price Index
2   i.e. structures that utilise borrowing
3   These include 2000, 2001, 2002 and 2008

Other Fast strategies do involve individual stocks. With rapid economic growth being a trend up to 2007, there have been plenty of opportunities for companies to grow rapidly. Those which have grown the fastest have normally been rewarded with high share prices, so there has been a tendency for investors to seek those businesses expanding most rapidly. Many companies have taken advantage of the low cost of debt to increase their borrowing, as this gives the impression of faster rates of growth. Others have grown into the fast growing emerging economies. This trend has been evident for so long that the largest quoted companies in the UK are now dominated by many stocks that fit into this category. Businesses that preferred to play a more conservative strategy have generally been acquired by either the more-borrowed companies, or by private equity investors, who also use very high levels of debt to enhance return.

With so many profitable capital gain strategies available, there has been a large increase in the number of market participants. More participants lead to more trading, and the average trading volume in the FTSE100 has approximately tripled between 1993 and 2010 to around £700m-£900 m each day.[4] Overall during the period of the credit boom, there has been a heavy skew of assets allocated to Fast strategies. Indeed, with the markets now crowded with Fast finance participants, what can be the advantage of turning back to review investment strategies of the past? How can a strategy like Graham's, published over fifty years ago, be relevant?

Old thinking in the new economy

The Intelligent Investor[5] is one of the first books that offered practical strategies as to how to minimise risk and maximise success in the art of investing. Part of this book's 'evergreen' success has been that the premium returns on its main strategy relied on some straightforward logic. In addition, Graham's principles were designed to work well even in the absence of an overall market rise. The strong rise in asset prices over the last twenty-five years is not 'normal', but when the credit boom ends it can be expected that market trends will revert back to those more similar to Graham's time. Indeed, when the credit boom is past, successful investors will need to renew their focus on strategies that can outperform *even in flat equity markets*. In this regard *The Intelligent Investor* is something of a foundation to the principles

---

4   Bloomberg daily FTSE 100 trading volume not available prior to 1993

5   Graham, B (1986) *The Intelligent Investor* 4th edition, Harper & Row

of Slow Finance. After all, how many investors do you know that use credit to enhance returns in the Japanese equity market? Perhaps it won't be long before Fast finance strategies go out of fashion, while Graham's ideals can be expected to become more relevant to investors in the modern age.

So what are Graham's three principles? Chapter Three has already touched on one – that of knowing what kind of investor you are. In modern terminology, they are the **Growth** Investors; often highly speculative and relying heavily on capital gain to make their return. The **Value** Investor, who seeks to invest in those companies that are out-of-fashion, which are often generating stable cash flow but modest growth. And the Index Plus or **Index** Investor that holds a good spread of both Growth and Value investments. Graham's guiding principle was to help investors avoid being caught out with sizable capital losses because a growth investment had disappointed. He believed that offering practical strategies to allocate capital to Value investments had a greater chance of success given that the capital could be left in place for an extended period without excessive risk. This chapter deals with two core methods that Graham believed would encourage these investor habits that delivered above average returns.

• Planning for stock market volatility and profiting from it;
• Always investing in companies with a margin of safety.

With recent market volatility in mind, both these themes seem highly pertinent today.

How to profit from market volatility

Graham was especially aware that uncertainty goes hand in hand with stock market investing. Even when the prospects of the underlying operations of a company did not change in an economic crisis, there is no guarantee the share price would not fall back sharply. So, however good the process of selecting the individual investments, the movement of the wider stock market could lead to sizable capital losses. Worse still, if the stock was popular, its share price could continue to fall for quite some time to a base price that might be a fraction of the original purchase price. The volatility of stock markets in the last ten years highlights this risk well. Sometimes markets react to the slightest tremors, but at other times they remain unchanged in the face of what appears to be a stream of bad news, before later experiencing wild fluctuations. Graham argued it was essential for the investor to plan for this kind of volatility, and to use this to their advantage.

To profit from market setbacks, Graham advised increasing the allocation of capital to equity investments at times of fear. This meant these bigger holdings could then enjoy the subsequent share price recovery and be sold when the holdings became relatively expensive. Therefore *The Intelligent Investor* recommends that investors do not invest all of their investment capital in stock market companies. Rather that they hold a mix of both stocks and defensive assets such as government bonds. For Graham, defensive assets included government bonds or cash. The twenty-first century investor has a wider range of 'defensive' assets to consider than his predecessor in the last century. Corporate bonds are normally more defensive than company shares. Large international companies are often perceived as having the advantage of deriving their cash-flow from a number of different countries and geographies. However government bonds have the advantage that they can increase the tax take on their local population, which a commercial organisation cannot. Another 'defensive' asset that is often popular in difficult times is gold bullion. Since there is no annual income on gold, and its price often moves like a commodity, most investors do not allocate a large proportion of their defensive assets to gold.

Graham advised a range of between twenty-five per cent and seventy-five per cent in equities and defensive assets respectively, with the percentages varying this over time based on the market movements. If the ratio was fifty/fifty initially, then when the stock market fell back, the investor has the advantage of sustaining a larger part of their investment capital than they would if it had all been allocated to the stock market. In fact, bonds often rise at times of distress, as they did in the economic crisis of 2008. So this strategy has the advantage of investors' capital being protected to a degree from the losses at times of market downturns.

The second aspect of Graham's strategy is even more important. He believed that investors should sell defensive assets and allocate towards additional stock market holdings at times of market distress. When the market recovered, the investor would have larger holdings in the intrinsically cheap stocks that recovered. To profit from market volatility, the investor needs to allocate capital to equities from bonds at times when the stock market is low. At times when the market is riding high, the opposite strategy should be employed, since presumably there are fewer stocks that are undervalued in an absolute sense.

Given that the Intelligent Investor is unlikely to transact just when the equity market is at its lowest point, Graham recommended a series of transactions to make the change, maybe over a few weeks or a few months. This is known as Pound-Cost Averaging and the details are outlined in Appendix 5. This investment strategy could have been highly successful over the years prior to the credit crunch. An overweight position in defensive assets would have been allocated, possibly in quite a large percentage change, in to equities some time during the second half of 2008, and this decision would have enhanced return substantially with stock market recovery in 2009/10.

Some may feel that a strategy with a maximum weighting of 75 per cent in shares is too conservative. During the credit boom a lot of investors have allocated almost all of their investment capital to assets that were highly volatile. The problem is that those who do hold bonds rarely make significant changes to the bond allocation at times of market distress. Graham's strategy heavily relies upon investors changing the allocation to equities and defensive assets, otherwise there is no way to profit from the market volatility.

It is worth remembering that Graham's philosophy was first to preserve capital and then find ways to make it grow. To contextualise, this strategy was proposed after the 1929 market crash, through the troubles of the 1930s, and the economic hardship of the Second World War. Hence, it was intentionally risk sensitive. The changes the allocation of cash/bonds could be as low as 25 per cent but also as high as 75 per cent. The *Intelligent Investor*, and indeed the *Slow Finance* investor, surely welcomes dips in the overall stock market, since this increases the chances of investing in stocks that are intrinsically cheap. But in fact there are very few investment managers who are willing to change their percentage of defensive assets significantly, and for this reason it is hard to sustain the charge that Graham is overly conservative.

For an individual investor, having some reserve capital in bonds (or other defensive assets) fits well with the principles of Slow Investment. It reduces the risk of the overall capital pool falling in value, and it enables the investor to take good advantage of the volatility of markets, to enhance their return. Whilst the principles of *Slow Finance* are mainly applicable to investment in stock market companies, the idea of having some degree of redundancy in the strategy exactly matches some of the issues noted in Chapter Two.

Invest in companies with a margin of safety

The second principle Graham advocated was buying stocks that are intrinsically cheap. In simple terms, Graham's goal was to buy assets worth £1 for 50 pence. This simple statement illustrates the **margin of safety**: the principle of buying shares in a quoted company at a significant discount to their intrinsic value. This principle offers the investor two possible benefits. First, should stock markets subsequently take a turn for the worse, then the further fall in the share price should only be temporary. Second, in time it might be anticipated that the share price of an intrinsically cheap company might recover back towards fair value, and that process should offer the scope for a premium return.

The key, of course, is how to judge intrinsic cheapness, to identify when a share price is good value. Graham identified two main criteria:

Reliability of earnings

He sought reliable businesses with unexceptional but consistent earnings prospects, over the long-term. This strategy sought to take advantage of the fact that speculative or growth investors overlooked more mundane business when investing. These businesses sometimes had the advantage of sustaining growth and excess cash for a much longer duration than the valuation discounted.

Where the tangible assets exceed the value of the business itself

There are some businesses where the share price is lower than the underlying asset value. Most often this is where the share price is below the value of the assets in the business, which is known as the book value. In some extreme cases the market capitalisation[6] is less than the cash held by the company on the balance sheet. Graham particularly liked these 'net nets' – where the cash in the business was worth more than the business itself. This effectively meant that Graham was buying the operational businesses for nothing. In Graham's time there were more of these around than in the modern markets. Graham passionately believed that the owner of shares should regard them first and foremost as conferring part ownership of the underlying business. With that in mind, the *stock owner* should not be too concerned with erratic fluctuations in stock prices, which are inevitable. Graham wrote: 'In the short term, the *stock market* behaves like a voting machine, but in the long term it acts like a weighing

---

6   Stock market value

machine.'[7] So whilst a share price might fall out of favour in terms of votes, in time the true intrinsic worth of the business will become the ultimate driver of share price. Graham's margin of safety worked in the same way.

This strategy fits well with the principles of Slow Finance. The investment decision is not driven by any upward momentum of the share price, or an anticipation that the business will grow fast in a coming time period. It is made on the basis of buying the investment when it is out-of-fashion, and then sitting back and waiting for this to change. The second principle of Slow Finance promotes investment simplicity. Companies that meet the margin of safety test are relatively easy to identify. Principle seven suggests that the investors are not guided by issues such as which index the stock is in, but be highly selective over those companies they want to support. This strategy is Slow.

Buying companies for less than their intrinsic worth is known as **Value investing**. Graham was the first to explicitly identify this approach. Graham defined an intrinsically cheap stock in absolute terms; one where the value of the tangible assets and cash within the business were above the stock market value (also known as the market capitalisation). The logic was that if the assets in the business were above the market capitalisation, and the company continued in business, then the market position of the business was likely to be valued at a higher level in time. This could come about as demand in the company's underlying markets improved, or with the arrival of a new management team. On top of this, if the business was liquidated, then after the sale of the business assets, the investor should still see a positive return. So making an investment on a Graham's intrinsic value basis met the purpose of the first principle, margin of safety.

The investor was unlikely to lose out by holding a Value investment whatever the stock market conditions, and they might get very lucky in terms of the upside potential. Over the last twenty-five years, some have suggested that modern strategies have left Graham's principle behind. After all, when Graham wrote his book he was interested in making *absolute* gains on his investments, whereas most asset allocators are now more interested in *relative* returns.

However in spite of the credit boom, Growth strategies have had times when expectations have been disappointed. Good examples are after the dotcom boom ended in 2000, and more recently with the credit crunch in

---

7   Graham, B (2008) *Security Analysis* 6th edition, McGraw-Hill Professional

2008. There is no problem with Graham's approach other than it is based on absolutes, so after the stock market took off in the 1980s most stocks traded at above their intrinsic worth for most of the period up to 2000. His strategy, based purely upon buying stocks that were intrinsically cheap, would have offered no real stock investment opportunities for perhaps a fifteen-year period.

For this reason, some question whether the strategy has added value. It is near impossible to check in retrospect because it is difficult to identify after the event the exact times that someone following the Graham intrinsic value strategy would have allocated capital out of bonds and into equities. Modern market participants are more interested in finding ways to outperform through the stock market cycles. If Graham's Value stocks could be defined in *relative*, not absolute terms, then investors could select their holdings from these, and still be investing with a margin of safety. Albeit a margin of relative safety rather than absolute safety. An updated strategy has the advantage of offering participation in markets irrespective whether the underlying stocks were actually as cheap as Graham would have liked them. So even during the 17-year market rise to 2000, it would have been possible for the Value Investor to remain invested and participate in the rising stock markets at that time. Of course, in contrast to Graham, those investing in relative value stocks would have also participated in the market setback in 2008.

The question is, how much does the Graham process offer in terms of outperformance through the stock market cycle? Should an investor applying the Slow Principles seek to select investments from those stocks that fall into the relative Value criteria? The theory that underpins this debate is very important in economics, since it is related to the idea that profitability of companies tends to revert to industry norms over time and under competitive conditions.[8] In fact, in the 1960s the Nobel Prize winning economist George Stigler called this one of the most important propositions in economic theory. He suggested that an industry front-runner is unlikely to stay in the lead forever, as its competitors either rush to catch up, or risk going out of business. Taken to its logical conclusion, stock market investors need to decide if they should be looking to buy shares in industry leaders, which will tend to be expensive, or the also-rans, which will tend to be cheap but may catch up in time. Put simply: should investors buy Growth or Value?

---

8   Stigler, G (1963) cited in *Wall Street Journal* Smart Money 07.04.11

Evaluating Value investing

Given the choice of investing in an industry leader or backing an improving tail-ender, many investors logically anticipate that the company with the stronger market position sustains the advantage. Assessing whether this is the best route to follow over a long time period is an important issue for investors, and has been the subject of a great deal of research. Work from eminent economists, repeated in a number of studies, has revealed an important conclusion. **History says that you should avoid the current market leader and pick the *less* fashionable stock to make the best investment return.**

The conclusions, based on the analysis of different periods of historic stock market data, demonstrate that investing in a stock market pool of **relative Value** stocks outperforms the stock market pool of **relative Growth** stocks. (See Appendix 4 for methodology.) Of course, there are years when relative Growth outperforms relative Value; indeed there can be runs of a number of years when this occurs. But, over time, the underlying trend always seems to reassert itself.

The studies covering the longest time period are probably the most interesting. Of course, investors are told all the time that past investment performance is no guide to the future, but analysing very long data ranges places what we know in context. The longer the time series, the greater the chance that trends can be anticipated to some degree. The longest running time series study in the US, published by Fama and French, and later joined by James Davies, was published in February 2000 in the *Journal of Finance*.[9] Their study examined prices on the New York Stock Exchange between 1929 and 1997, recalculating the relative value of each stock every year, and then measured the differential in performance of the relative Value group against the relative Growth group.

On average, Value stocks outperformed Growth stocks by between 0.4 and 0.5 per cent *each month*.

This is a very convincing conclusion. Not only does it reinforce Graham's general recommendation, but also it shows that this relationship has remained in place in the decades following the publication of *The Intelligent Investor* – including some of the period of the credit boom. The study did note that the Value Effect was a little greater in the period up to 1963 than in the data from 1963 to 1997. There were periods when Growth companies

---

9   Davies, J.L, Fama, E.F, French, K.R (2000) *Characteristics, Covariances and Average Returns 1929–1997* Journal of Finance LV (1)

as a group recovered some lost ground to Value stocks. Overall, however, the trend was for Value to outperform, and the evidence is that Graham's principle remains valid even in modern times. This is a very important conclusion for Slow Investors. This data series has subsequently been updated on an annual basis, and the same trends broadly persist.

The overall outperformance of the relative Value stocks over the relative Growth stocks is 3.3 per cent a year.[10]

Fig 4.1: Different Investment Styles
Cumulative returns from value, 'middling' and growth strategies
US equities 1926-2010

2010

Value

$21,815

Middling

$2,340

Growth

$1,417

1926

$1 Invested

Classification according to book-to-market ratio;
monthly returns compounded over time.

Source: Professor Kenneth French, Tuck School of Business, Dartmouth (website)

---

10 Fama, E.F, French, K.R (2007) *The Anatomy of Value & Growth Stock Returns* Financial Analysts Journal 63(6) pp. 44–55

In the UK, a team of professors have compiled an even more extensive data set than in the US. Professors Elroy Dimson, Paul Marsh and Mike Staunton work together at London Business School. They have compiled an archive of UK stock market data from 1900 to 2010 that is the longest of its kind in the world. However the series does not have book values of many of the stocks in the early time periods. For this reason, the professors have used a different method to identify investments with relatively high value per share.

There is good evidence that the ability to pay **good levels of dividends** compared with the market capitalisation is an equally good measure of value as the ratio of book value of assets to market capitalisation.[11] Whichever method of value is used to determine the intrinsic underlying value in a quoted business, the results are broadly consistent with the US study. It seems there is much to recommend a value-based investment strategy, favouring companies which have a higher level of book assets compared with other alternative quoted companies. In normal stock market conditions, the relative value strategy is likely to be successful.

Investors should allocate capital to Value stocks in preference to Growth stocks, building in the prospect of improved portfolio returns in the longer term.

Reconnecting and taking control

There is good news for the individual investor in all of this. The Slow Investor can apply this strategy even without relying wholly upon the funds offered by the professional fund managers. Davies, Fama and French's conclusions demonstrate there are anomalies in the stock market that can be exploited just as successfully by the individual as the large professional fund.

This book also advocates that Index investors move to reconnect, taking a greater interest in how their savings are allocated between Growth and Value investment portfolios. In the credit boom, many institutions increased their allocation of assets to large and international quoted companies, the beneficiaries of lower borrowing costs, and reduced their allocation to small and local companies. In an environment of ample credit, and in a globalised world, large players were winners. Yet long-term

---

11 Reviewed in Chapter 5

investment data, stretching over a century in the UK, suggests that this may not be the most effective strategy in the years ahead.

Index Plus or Index investors, including those saving through their corporate pension scheme, have a real interest in how well the underlying assets perform. In previous decades, the majority of pension investment schemes offered a Defined Benefit (DB) based upon a percentage of the participant's salary. If the assets in such schemes performed really well, then the scheme could offer improved pension terms to the investor. For this reason, even participants in DB pension schemes have a direct interest in the overall return of their assets.

It is now more common for pensions to be offered on a Defined Contribution (DC) basis, with the individual and the employer making regular payments to the scheme. The ultimate pension payments to the scheme member are determined by the capital sum accrued at the time of retirement. And many of those with DB or DC schemes are choosing to move their capital to a Self Invested Pension Plan.

For Index investors who allocate their stock market savings directly, there are investment products specifically run to meet these requirements. Equity Index funds replicate a particular index, most commonly the most well-known such as the FTSE 100, or the FTSE All Share. Typically Index funds charge very low annual management fees so the fund itself generates a return very close to that of an Index. The problem lies in the fact that the most well-known indices do not have a Value bias. It is difficult for the Index Investor to allocate assets to a Value strategy in line with the Graham thesis.

As the credit boom comes to an end, there is a greater need for the individual to identify an investment strategy that offers the prospect of a premium return, albeit with a margin of safety. And even if the pension investor chooses to take an Index stance, it involves firstly considering the mix of equities and more defensive assets, and that those ratios are readjusted when following periods of differential movement. Whatever the pension arrangements of the individual, there is a much greater responsibility for individuals to take a greater interest in the investment markets and make informed decisions about how their assets are allocated.

In my view, Graham's principle of selecting investments with a margin of safety *is* likely to be successful, though in its absolute form it has the disadvantage of potentially leaving a large part of the investor's capital sitting in defensive assets during the best of the stock markets moves. For that reason, the strategy of relative Value[12] has been developed. This has delivered premium returns in the past, even during the recent credit boom, though to a lesser degree. If the current credit boom is indeed coming to an end, then it is likely that the relative Value strategy could enjoy a period of catch up to the long-term trend of outperformance. Ideally it should be used with Graham's strategy of holding a significant portion of savings in defensive assets, which might include government bonds, cash, – or even for the most conservative – gold bullion.

The Slow Investor can build on the foundation established by Benjamin Graham. It is possible to invest appropriately with a margin of safety, knowing that the strategy has been tested in both up and down markets. It is very interesting that forgoing the opportunities of investing in the fastest growth companies does not disadvantage those with a Slow mindset. Conversely, it is an investment strategy based upon buying into the unfashionable business with consistent but unremarkable prospects that delivers sizable premium returns to the long term investor. It seems that the principles have been delivering premium returns for many decades. It is only the excitement of the Growth strategies that has obscured thinking, and meant that investors have failed to embrace the Slow perspective.

---

12 Calculated using the book value of the assets compared to the overall market capitalisation of the company

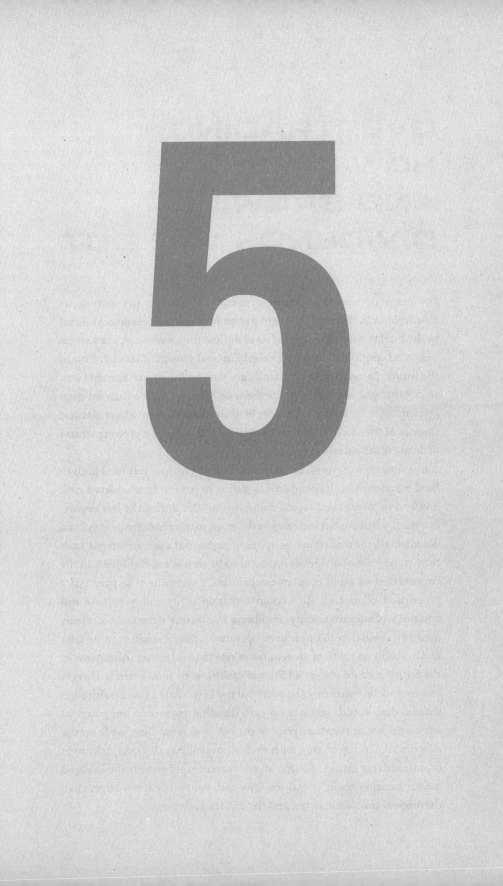

OVERTRADING: HOW GOOD AND GROWING DIVIDENDS WIN OUT

For many decades, how much a company chose to pay out to its shareholders in dividends has sent out an important psychological signal to the market about the scale of its cash flow from current operations, as well as its confidence in the sustainability and growth of its cash flow in the future. In many ways dividends are vital to long-term shareholders, since otherwise the only way for them to receive a cash return on their investment is by selling a portion of their shareholding. Many classical theories of the stock market are based upon the value of a growing stream of dividends to shareholders.

In a slow growth world, the cash flow from a business was used both to fund the growth of the company, as well as to pay its shareholders a cash dividend to justify their capital commitment. But during the last twenty-five years, when annual increases in the stock market have frequently been double-digit, the traditional discipline of paying out a part of internal cash flow in the form of dividends has come to be seen as old-fashioned. In the environment of rapid economic expansion, a company that paid out a proportion of its cash flow could constrain in its ability to take full advantage of buoyant trading conditions. In contrast, if the same company used *all* its cash flow to invest in its operations, then it could grow its sales and probably its profit at an even faster rate than otherwise. Alternatively, the business could use its additional cash flow to fund interest charges and repay debt, enhancing the potential rise in its share price. So although shareholders would miss out on cash dividend payments, the potential additional rise in the share price of the business more than made up the differential. On top of this, with the easy availability of credit, takeovers became easier to finance. So after several years of rapid growth, the enlarged market position could be realised for a cash sum many times larger than the original cost of the shares and the dividends forgone.

As a result, many investors preferred to defer their cash dividends during the credit boom, in favour of those businesses that retained all their earnings and were expected to make a better return through a capital gain. Share prices discounted the better capital gain prospects of very fast-growing companies, with valuations that were often considerably higher than more ordinary stocks. Smaller businesses that persisted with good and growing dividend payments were often perceived to be slightly stubborn, and there was a suspicion over whether they really had good enough growth potential, given that they didn't need all their internal cash flow to fund it. So a company that paid out decent dividends was perceived to be giving a signal to shareholders that they were more of a modest growth business. The stock market therefore priced it on a modest valuation, exactly the *opposite* of the normal position when those with good and growing dividends were often rated the most highly. This process actively discouraged dividend payments, since to pay dividends suggested the modest growth ambitions of the management, penalising their cost of capital. Often the re-listing of a smaller company from the Main List on the London Stock Exchange to the Alternative Investment Market (AIM),[1] the market for growth companies, was accompanied with a cessation of the previous dividend policy. New listings often followed the same trend and came to market with a policy of paying zero dividends.

This trend became so endemic that by the start of 2011, around three-quarters of companies quoted on AIM did not pay dividends.[2] This did reflect the fact that many AIM companies are still in start-up mode, where their operations require ongoing cash investment. In these cases, dividend payments would be inappropriate. In addition, around a third of companies quoted on AIM are resources stocks. These companies plan to develop a valuable oil or mineral resource in the future by investing capital in development projects over the coming years. Again since most of these businesses require sizable cash investments, dividend payments are again inappropriate.

However, aside from the examples above, there are a very large number of AIM-listed companies that are trading successfully, operating at a profit, generating surplus cash with strong balance sheets but still do not pay dividends. They wish to be seen as businesses with excellent growth

---

1   Alternative Investment Market: London's international market for small & growing companies
2   Source: Financial Times 18.05.2011 *Desire for dividends outweighs capital growth* David Blackwell

potential; so paying out dividends may be misinterpreted by investors as a sign of management lacking in growth ambition. But when the attitude of investors changes to favour the Slow agenda, then these AIM-listed companies may be particularly well-placed to take advantage of the new trend. Not only would they be able to resume dividend payments at good levels of initial yield, but also those with good prospects may also be able to provide a growing level of dividend. This combination would be especially attractive given the constrained returns available in most other asset classes.

Many profitable companies in the stock market are valued on a Price/ Earnings Ratio (PER).[3] However it is possible to invert this ratio, making it the Earnings/Price Ratio (EPR).[4] This calculates the amount the company might be able to pay out in dividends if it paid out all of its earnings. For example, a business on a PER of 8, would be able to pay a maximum dividend yield of one eighth of its share price or 12.5 per cent. Of course no business could afford to invest nothing in its future operations, or pay out 100 per cent of its earnings, but this is a quick method of working out just how much dividend yield might come out of a business for shareholders. The ratio is technically known as the Earnings Yield.[5] In the past, many companies had a policy of distributing around one third of their earnings in dividend; one third of the 12.5 per cent earnings yield is just over 4 per cent so that might be the dividend yield of such a business. Some companies can afford to invest rather less in the business, and may pay out one half of their earnings. In that case, the dividend yield to shareholder would be around 6.25 per cent, being exactly half of 12.5 per cent earnings yield.

Slow Finance anticipates that investor desire for dividends will become re-established, bringing it back in line with the previous standing. The adoption of *Slow Finance* principles will be a major shift in attitude for investors who have previously been accustomed to chasing quick share price moves. Substantial wealth can be built with greater certainty, and slowly through receiving dividends over longer time periods rather than by pursuing fast changing fashions for capital gains. Since the level of the dividend set by a company reflects its confidence about the sustainability

---

3   Valuation ratio calculated by dividing share price by earnings per share (EPS)

4   Earnings per share (EPS) over 12 months divided by share price

5   Calculated by dividing earnings per share over 12 months by share price

of cash flow into the future, then it can be seen why shareholders may once again focus heavily upon this aspect when allocating capital.

Size: understanding dividend payout strategies

When it comes to larger companies, investors clearly do not expect out-and-out growth. The law of large numbers highlights that a very large company cannot keep doubling in size since theoretically it would then become larger than the world economy. As larger businesses are not expected to grow as rapidly as smaller ones, it is more usual for them to generate excess cash and, in the absence of rapid growth, pay this out as dividends (even during a credit boom). The problems of the credit crunch did upset the apple cart for some. In particular, the banks' urgent need for additional capital led to most of their dividends being suspended, and this was often accompanied by a call to raise more capital via one or more sizeable rights issues.[6] A similar pattern was seen in some other companies, including some insurance businesses and property companies, most particularly those carrying a great deal of debt. More recently, the costs of the giant BP oil spill in the Gulf of Mexico led to it suspending its dividend payment for three quarters, although it has since been re-initiated at half the previous level. The overall pattern in UK dividend income was that the payments provided by the stock market fell back after the credit crunch of 2008 and have not recovered much since then.

The reduction of income possibilities has been reflected in other asset classes as well. Bond prices have been raised by the operation of QE, so to gain reasonable income levels investors need to buy bonds with relatively long duration which incurs volatility risks. Even so, bonds do not offer any prospect of income growth other than in the case of the low yield inflation-adjusted bonds. Corporate bonds are broadly similar. Now that property rental levels have recovered after the deep recession of 2008/09, few expect any meaningful growth in rental levels either. So it may be that, aside from certain equities, there's almost *no* opportunity for investors to identify investments with attractive income growth.

Given large companies' dependence on overall world growth, in the post credit boom period it may be difficult to grow profits and earnings in a

---

6 Rights issue: Offer to existing shareholders to buy stock at a given price, often at a discount, within a fixed time period

meaningful way. Indeed, it is possible to anticipate that the earnings yield of many larger companies could be all but stagnate. Larger businesses may be poorly positioned to grow their dividends meaningfully, possibly for an extended period. Smaller businesses face different challenges. Given that smaller businesses pay few dividends, there is little risk of shareholders being heavily disappointed from here with regard to income distribution. The onset of credit constraint may not seem the moment for companies to start increasing payouts. Indeed, in the last few years, many smaller companies have felt even less sure about their access to bank credit, and therefore may be even less inclined to pay out dividends to shareholders.

But the onset of credit constraint may change attitudes in the financial sector. Smaller businesses may find that the availability of bank credit could actually *improve* for them in the coming years. This may seem perverse, but it relates to the lack of credit available for smaller quoted companies recently. During the credit boom, banks mainly concentrated on supplying the larger blocks of credit, which mainly suited medium and larger sized businesses. Bigger tickets meant bigger profits. During the last twenty years the corporate bond market has grown rapidly in the UK, displacing demand for overdrafts and fixed term borrowing from medium and larger corporates. Bank managers were retired as the scale of the traditional corporate overdrafts market shrank to a very small part of a bank's operations. This process of 'crowding out' corporate fixed-term loans and overdrafts actually inhibited the ability of smaller business access to borrowing. Although borrowing was plentiful in the credit boom, it was the large clients who enjoyed the commercial advantage. Subsequently, with the first onset of the financial crisis, banks were forced to shrink their balance sheet commitments and so all parts of the bank saw a withdrawal of most loans that were not essential. Consequently, at the end the credit boom, many small quoted companies ended up with deleveraged balance sheets. As recently as February 2011, Barclays announced it was withdrawing from the corporate leasing market, presumably because the scale of its profits are too small in the context of the whole group.[7]

Financial attitudes can be expected to change, and this could include the banks' attitude towards lending to quoted smaller companies. It seems it is only a question of when. Small quoted companies are some of the best quality customers for borrowing that banks can find. They are generally

---

7   See Leasing World *Barclays cuts asset finance to SMEs* 16.02.11

simple to comprehend, borrow relatively modestly, and can normally raise additional monies if they run short of capital. When the credit boom ends, it is likely that the demand for credit from businesses with good chances of repaying will all but dry up. This effect has already been seen across Europe. Those banks that have spare lending capacity will realise that the most urgent borrowers are those that have poor chances of repaying in full, being already overgeared, or otherwise in trouble. Banks will then remember why prior to the credit boom they used to lend more willingly to smaller businesses that had a sustained cash flow and the ability to raise additional capital.

In a world where many have borrowed too much, small and micro-quoted businesses[8] that show sustained cash generation could be reassessed as highly attractive customers. They may be small and fiddly, but even that could work in their advantage as each sum at risk would be relatively small. So, perversely, smaller quoted companies may find that their access to credit actually improves in the coming period. This would amount to a reversal of the trend seen during the credit boom. Meanwhile those businesses still growing their sales and profits would be likely to be doing so at a slower rate. Profitable businesses wouldn't need to retain all their earnings since there will be less need to invest so heavily in new capacity or to fund additional working capital. As a result, many smaller quoted companies may find themselves with increased liquidity after the credit boom.

The previous section concluded that shareholders may once again focus heavily upon good and growing dividends when allocating capital. This section concludes that some small quoted businesses will be in a position where they have been under-distributing in dividends during the credit boom, but may be unusually well placed to resume paying good and growing income. Given the comparative rarity of alternative investments in the future, this change might have a profound effect on the valuations of smaller quoted businesses. Given that smaller quoted companies by their nature are limited in scale, it's possible that demand for these investments could be large in relation to the overall scale of the stock available, and therefore the price appreciation might be fairly sizable. A wide range of investors might be inclined to chase the bandwagon, in a universe that itself may already be outperforming.

---

8   Small & micro-cap: Small and very small in terms of market capitalisation. Size is defined relative to other listed stocks, not in absolute terms

The compounding effect of good and growing dividends

For those looking for a sustained income from their savings, it's obvious why a good and growing dividend would be attractive. Inflation tends to rise and, all things being equal, most individuals would aim for their annual expenditure to rise progressively each year, even if their purchasing habits did not change. But is there any benefit to shareholders if a business pays dividends? Surely cash in the business belongs to the shareholders irrespective of whether it is paid out or retained in the company, in the same way that dividends belong to the shareholders?

A number of studies have been carried out on whether it is more attractive for companies to reinvest their surplus cash in their own businesses or whether it is better for the investor to receive a dividend payment and use it to buy more shares.[9] Both strategies have advantages and disadvantages, but ultimately it boils down to how well the business is doing. A very successful business can gain great advantage by reinvesting internal cash flow. If that cash was paid out as a dividend, then it's likely that the investor may suffer a tax liability and pay a premium valuation to buy more shares given the share price would reflect the strong prospects for the business. If the company was growing rapidly then it might find it needed additional capital, and might choose to raise additional capital from its shareholders. So paying out cash to shareholders in dividends and later asking for more cash to fund the business could be seen as inconsistent by some.

I don't find it inconsistent. In the pre-credit boom days, investors expected a return for the risk capital they put up to support a business. Although the stock market does appreciate over the very long term, for extended periods it can trade broadly sideways,[10] so the appreciation of a share price is not a reliable way of securing a return on risk capital. In contrast, a semi-annual cash payment from the business in the form of a dividend offers a regular return (other than when the business hits a major setback). Prior to the credit boom, those companies that paid a good and growing dividend yield moved to valuation premiums. The business funding the acquisition would

9   Miller, H.M, Modigliani, F (1961) *Dividend Policy, Growth and The Valuation of Shares* Journal of Business, (34) pp. 411–433; Black, F (1976) *The Dividend Puzzle* The Journal of Portfolio Management (**4**) pp. 634–639

10   i.e. trade within a relatively narrow range

have a lower cost of equity.[11] Of even greater importance, these companies also found that shareholders were more inclined to support share issues so the business was in an advantageous position to acquire distressed assets when most others could not, possibly at a knock down price. Acquisitions made on this basis often have a very much higher rate of return that those made when many other corporates are able to fund them. So my view is that dividends are highly valued by investors in preference to cash being retained in the company, certainly at times when market conditions are not buoyant.

Therefore in normal market conditions, there are arguments for suggesting that paying attractive dividends may be beneficial to quoted businesses. But what if you are an investor who is saving for the long-term future, and are disinterested as to whether they receive return in capital or income accumulation? Would shares offering good and growing dividends be attractive compared with those that may offer greater prospects of capital gains? A worked example of a quoted company paying a sustained and modestly growing dividend and compared with a business that retains all its earnings can help clarify the differences.

Fig 5.1: The power of compounding
A decade of reinvesting a 5% dividend yielder each year

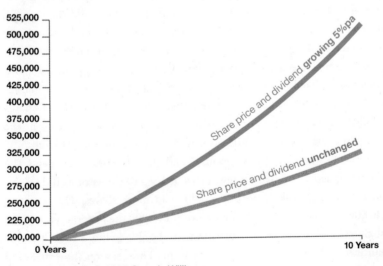

Source: Copyright © 2011 Gervais Williams

---

11 Cost of equity: The return required by shareholders for investing in a company to reflect compensation for the risks of ownership

We'll assume the business operates in the same way, irrespective of the potential extra capital retained in the business that chooses not to pay dividends. Often prudent rates of investment growth can be funded by a business following either policy. Moreover, one-off peaks in investment spend can be funded by borrowings that are inexpensive, if used in moderation.

Suppose an investor who doesn't need immediate income invests in a company that does not pay a dividend. They would hold a fixed percentage of the company, and if the company was successful, then the investor would participate in that success in a similar way to all other shareholders through a potential share price rise. If the company decided to pay out dividends each year, the business might continue to be just as successful, but the investor may reinvest those dividends buying more shares in the company, or use the dividend income for other investments. The reinvesting of dividend income to buy more shares in the business would in this instance give the investor an increased percentage shareholding in the business, albeit one that has a little less cash on the balance sheet compared to the earlier example.

A company making £3 million a year of pre-tax profit would earn £2 million per year after tax (if it paid tax of 33 per cent on its earnings). If it retained £1 million in the business to fund growth, it could then pay £1 million to investors in dividends. Shareholders with a 1 per cent holding would receive 1 per cent of £1 million, or £10,000. Potential tax payments would complicate the calculation but are ignored for simplicity. On a valuation of ten times annual post-tax earnings, the total market capitalisation would be £20 million, so buying £10,000 worth of shares would increase the investor original shareholding from 1 per cent of the company, i.e. £200,000, to 1.05 per cent of the company, or £210,000.

If the business traded sideways,[12] and paid the same dividend the following year as it did in the previous year, then the investor would receive an increased dividend, since it would hold more shares. The dividend cheque would be £10,500, compared with £10,000 the previous year. If the share price were the same, they would also be able to buy a slightly larger number of shares than the previous year too. These figures show that even in a business that is not growing its dividend, for the shareholder who reinvests, dividend payments have some attractions.

---

12 Trading sideways: Trading within broadly the same range

Fig 5.2: Understanding investment

Much of the world of investment rests on a simple equation consisting of three parts: income, capital and yield. If you know two of these, you can instantly work out the third.

Where the income is constant (from government bonds, for example), if the yield falls, then the capital value must appreciate. For assets where the income stream can vary, the equation can be reversed: if the income stream grows and the yield remains constant, then the capital must appreciate. This is the theory that supports the long-term capital appreciation of equities.

The relationships between the three variables can be expected to shift over time according to the forces of supply and demand within the market.

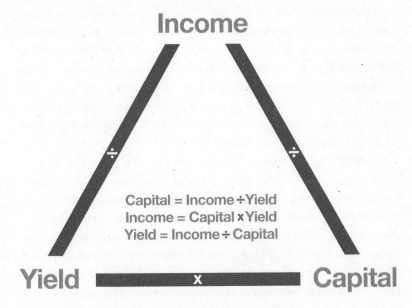

$$Capital = Income \div Yield$$
$$Income = Capital \times Yield$$
$$Yield = Income \div Capital$$

Source: Sarasin & Partners Compendium of Investment January 2010

This effect is called dividend compounding.[13] The example above only covers two years, and the compounding effect is fairly modest. But, over longer time periods, the effect can grow to make a very sizeable difference. For the example above, assuming the share price and dividend distribution didn't change, the investor's percentage of the company would grow from

---

13 Dividend compounding: Reinvesting dividend income from a stockholding back into buying more stock of the same company, increasing the overall size of the holding.

1 per cent in year one to 1.7 per cent of the business in year ten through dividend reinvestment. So the annual yield[14] on the original investment would have grown from £10,000 to £16,288 p.a., and the investor would hold shares valued at £325,778.

This is all very interesting but the same calculations apply to those holding bonds which typically have a constant level of interest payment. The point about equity investment is that the dividends can grow over time. The power of compounding works much more impressively in a business when it's growing its dividend payments. For if a company that has a dividend yield[15] of 5 per cent grows its income by 5 per cent per year, the maths becomes compelling. And if the dividend yield on the shares remains constant, then each year the share price will rise by 5 per cent as the dividend payment rises by 5 per cent, 5 per cent in income and 5 per cent in capital growth. Compounding at a 5 per cent increase in dividend a year would lead to the original investment having a running yield[16] of 25 per cent on the original cost of the investment after 10 years, and the capital value of the shares that originally cost £200,000 having a total value, including the income reinvested, of £518,748 after ten years. That is the true power of compounding.

Good and growing dividends are obviously highly attractive for those investors who need an annual income to cover their expenditure. But the calculations above also suggest such shareholdings are very attractive for those investors who can reinvest the dividends since the capital value either increases with the dividends, or if the share price remains stationary, compounds at an even faster rate. The power of compounding has generally been overlooked by most investors over the fast years of the credit boom. If the fast trend is coming to an end, then expect to hear a lot more about compounding in the future. Slow investors will have a strong interest in selecting investments with good and growing income.

The compounding effect and stock market indices

Stock market indices are used to give clients and investors a yardstick to assess how well their funds have performed. It's important that they reflect

---

14 Yield: Income return on an investment

15 Dividend yield: Ratio calculated by dividing dividend payments by share price

16 Running yield: Income return on an investment as a percentage of market value

the range of stocks available from which the investor can pick, and it is customary for indices to be defined by a geographical area. The most widely used in the UK is the FTSE All-Share Index, which was first compiled in the 1930s and is still calculated today. Clients and investors are also interested as to how different parts of the investment universe might be performing. Consequently, indices are often put together to cover just a part of the investment universe in a territory. In the UK there is the RBS Hoare Govett Smaller Companies (HGSC) index. RBS Securities is a stockbroker in London (formerly Hoare Govett) with a strong team specialising in the smaller quoted companies in the UK.

So how is the movement of an index calculated? During the year, the share price performance of each company can be measured. But it would be misleading if the movement of a stock market index were calculated by merely averaging the annual moves of all the small and large companies. If a tiny stock went up ten times one year, this would be insignificant for investors when compared to ten of the largest quoted companies whose stock fell by just 1 per cent. So the index returns are normally calculated using the percentage movement in each share price, weighted by the overall size of the individual company.

Small-cap companies with stock market quotations are not small in the sense of small private businesses such as the neighbourhood chemist or the local window-cleaner. In fact, many are very substantial operators in their markets. Compared to small private business, small quoted companies can be quite large. There is no formal definition of a small quoted company, but they are defined relative to the rest of the market, and larger quoted businesses.[17] The definition used in 1987 was that a small company was one that fell outside the aggregate value of the largest 90 per cent of those listed on the London Stock Exchange. By implication, this group comprises a tenth of the total value of all the quoted companies listed in London.

During 2010,[18] companies in the bottom 10 per cent of the stock market rose by an average of 26.4 per cent, which compares with a return on the FTSE All-Share index of just 14.5 per cent. 'Small' outperformed the market as a whole over this short time scale. That is certainly interesting for the Slow Investor.

---

17 Source: London Stock Exchange

18 Calendar year to Dec 2010

To keep the constituents of an index consistent in the longer term, at the end of each year the full universe of stocks listed in London is rebalanced to take account of those businesses that have exited or arrived on the stock market. Those that have grown to become too large or dropped into the bottom 10 per cent are reallocated each year into a new group for the index of large or small companies respectively for the coming year.

Index data regarding the performance of smaller businesses has been collected since 1987. In addition, data has been back-calculated to 1955. So how has the HGSC Index performed since 1955?[19] £1 invested at the start of 1955 in the average small company would have grown to a capital sum of £218 in 2010. This doesn't include any dividends that may have been paid. Fifty-six years is a very long investment period. Most of us will not hold our savings for anything like this length of time. However, the fact that an investment of £1 can grow to be worth £218 demonstrates why investing in small quoted companies is potentially attractive. It should be remembered that, with the rise of average prices, £1 today is only worth a small fraction of £1 in 1955, so the true capital gain in real terms (as economists call it) is rather less than two hundred times the original investment.

But what of the dividends? What difference have they made? Taking dividend income and reinvesting it by buying more shares has a very powerful compounding effect over a ten-year period, and it can be expected to have a much greater effect over a period of more than fifty years. And so it has. The accrued value of the original investment of £1 at the start of 1955, if invested in the average company in the smallest 10 per cent of the London Stock Market, with the dividends reinvested, would have grown to be worth £3,248 by 2010. Attractive, eh?

A strategy based on premium dividend yields

Chapter 4 has already explored why an investment strategy based upon **relative value** might be successful. It concluded that using the book value of the assets compared to the overall market capitalisation of the company had a good chance of offering premium returns. Now it's time to add another element to the tools that Slow investors might be interested in using in the search for premium returns.

---

19 Dimson, E, Marsh, P (2011) RBS HGSC Annual Report (2011) p. 22

Fig 5.3: The small company effect
Investing in the UK's smallest listed companies

2010
Micros
Capital gain plus dividends reinvested (DMS MicroCap index)

£14,210

Small
Capital gain plus dividends reinvested (RBS HGSC Index)

£3,248

Small
Capital gain only (RBS HGSC Index)

£218

1955
£1 Invested

Source: Elroy Dimson, Paul Marsh, Mike Staunton, London Business School, RBS Securities

Professors Elroy Dimson, Paul Marsh and Mike Staunton from the London Business School, believe that **the ability to pay a good dividend yield compared to market capitalisation is an equally good measure of relative value** as the book value measure.[20] If that is the case, the next

---

20 Dimson, E, Marsh, P, Stauton, M (2011) *Credit Suisse Global Investment Returns Yearbook* p. 19
    London Business School

question is whether this can help investors to select stocks that outperform over the longer term, and if so, by how much. Dimson *et al.* used the world's longest series of stock market data to investigate whether UK stocks characterised by good levels of dividend yield had outperformed lower yielding growth stocks, i.e. more expensive, fashionable shares in the last 111 years. Their analysis suggested that **relative value investments with good levels of dividend yield outperformed relative growth investments in the UK by an average of 2.9 per cent per year.**[21]

Fig 5.4: Investment returns 1900-2010
Cumulative return from low & high yielders within the top 100 UK stocks

2010
_____

High Yield

£100,160

Market Yield

£23,335

Low Yield
£5,122

1900
_____
£1 Invested

Source: Elroy Dimson, Paul Marsh and Mike Staunton, London Business School

This is another strong finding, which a Slow Investor can use to help in asset selection. Investors should note, though, that this long-run average is made up of some variable performance,[22] with growth stocks outperforming at certain times, including the credit-fuelled 1990s.

21 Dimson, E, Marsh, P, Stauton, M (2011) *Credit Suisse Global Investment Returns Sourcebook* pp. 45–46 London Business School

22 Dimson, E, Nagel, S & Quigley, G (2003) *Capturing the Value Premium in the UK* Financial Analysts Journal 59(6) pp. 35–45

In addition, the LBS professors turned back to the US, reworking data from the New York Stock Exchange analysed by Fama and French, again using premium dividend yield as the determinant of premium returns rather than book value.[23] The results suggested that relative value investments with good levels of dividend yield outperformed relative growth investments by 2.8 per cent per year on average between 1926 and 2010. Furthermore, it is reassuring to see that the two different methods of determining the relative value of underlying business have comparable returns. The professors state that: 'The yield premium is now widely viewed as a manifestation of the value effect.'[24]

There have been a number of studies that have sought to explain why such a consistent market anomaly persists. Put simply: why are growth stocks apparently delivering less impressive returns than the also-rans? Rob Arnott, Fei-Fei Li and Katrina Sherrerd published one of the most conclusive papers on the subject.[25] Generally, investors were successful at identifying those companies that were likely to grow at a faster rate in the future, but tended to overpay for those stocks. On some occasions they paid up to *twice* as much as was justified later by the actual return to shareholders. It seems that investors become over-enthused about companies with good prospects, and their share prices move up to valuations well above their long-term intrinsic value.[26]

> '...maybe, just maybe, investors will one day learn their lesson and stop rising to the bait of growth.'
>
> **Profs Elroy Dimson, Paul Marsh and Mike Staunton**,
> London Business School

The LBS professors have carried out similar studies to see if companies with a yield premium also outperform in many other countries' stock markets. The data series is naturally much shorter, but it still covers thirty-five years,

23 Dimson, E, Marsh, P, Stauton, M (2011) *Credit Suisse Global Investment Returns Yearbook* p. 19 London Business School

24 Dimson, E, Marsh, P, Stauton, M (2011) *Credit Suisse Global Investment Returns Yearbook* p. 19 London Business School

25 Arnott, A, Li, F, Sherrerd, K (2009) *Claivoyant Value and the Value Effect* Journal of Portfolio Management 35 pp. 12–26

26 Dimson, E, Marsh, P, Stauton, M (2011) *Credit Suisse Global Investment Returns Yearbook* p. 19 London Business School

from 1975 to 2010.[27] Readers will note that this period principally includes the credit boom, when in my view the trends in the stock market may have been abnormal. It is therefore no surprise to find that the returns on relative value strategies have been somewhat more erratic in this period.

The return on the relative value strategies in the nineteen countries studied (including the UK and the US) suggested that they added 2.5 per cent a year overall. However, during that period there were six countries where the relative value strategy underperformed. The most extreme example was Ireland, where relative growth stocks outperformed by 5.4 per cent a year! Meanwhile, the country where the relative value strategy was most successful was Japan where it outperformed by 6.2 per cent.[28]

Fig 5.5: The premium returns on various value strategies 1975-2010
Annualised value premiums in nineteen countries (%)

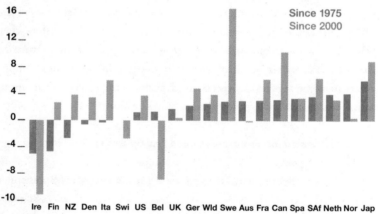

Source: Copyright © 2011 Elroy Dimson, Paul Marsh and Mike Staunton

The fact that these two countries had such contrasting results is entirely in line with the thesis that incidence of the credit boom has skewed the returns on the relative value strategy. Of the countries included in the study, Ireland is certainly the one where the credit boom had the greatest

---

27 Dimson, E, Marsh, P, Stauton, M (2011) *Credit Suisse Global Investment Returns Yearbook* p. 19 London Business School

28 Dimson, E, Marsh, P, Stauton, M (2011) *Credit Suisse Global Investment Returns Sourcebook* p. 47 London Business School

effect on its economy. In contrast, of all the countries studied, the Japanese economy seemed the least affected by the credit boom. Japanese economic growth has been very slow for the last twenty years or so since its period of rapid growth came to an end in 1990.

Finally, this study also examined whether the share prices of stocks with a premium yield moved less erratically than other stocks. Indeed they did. The share price of a business that suffers a setback in trading profits falls less fast if it sustains a significant dividend payment when compared to one that pays a smaller dividend payment, or that has no dividend payment at all.[29]

Investing for good and growing dividend income

There is a very substantial difference in index returns between those generated by a capital gain and those generated by the compounding of good and growing dividend income. During the excitement and high returns available throughout the period of the credit boom, the power of the compounding of dividend payments has seemed less important. If austerity budgets and credit constraint are a part of the future, then market indices may not deliver much capital return for an extended period. At these times, professional investors will need to find every possible way of enhancing return for clients, and dividend compounding can be expected to play a key part. In the coming decade, I believe that most investors will regard this as one of the most important aspects when selecting individual stocks for their portfolios; this is a key outcome of Slower finance.

Secondly, the paying of a premium dividend yield is an equally valid method of identifying stocks that are intrinsically undervalued by the stock market. An investment strategy based upon relative value, with individual investments selected via their premium yields, is likely to work well for Slow investors. This strategy has delivered premium returns in the past, particularly during periods other than credit booms. If the current credit boom is indeed coming to an end, then it's likely that a strategy based upon good and growing dividends will once again be successful.

Rather counter-intuitively, perhaps, Dimson, Marsh and Staunton are also convinced that higher yielding stocks actually deliver a better return

---

29 Dimson, E, Marsh, P, Stauton, M (2011) *Credit Suisse Global Investment Returns Yearbook* p. 20 London Business School

but do not necessarily imply a higher level of risk for investors. 'We have shown that, historically, investment strategies tilted towards higher-yielding stocks have generally proved profitable... While higher risk would seem an obvious explanation, our research indicates that portfolios of higher-yielding stocks have actually proved less risky than an equivalent investment in lower-yielding stocks...'[30]

Enough said.

30 Dimson, E, Marsh, P, Stauton, M (2011) *Credit Suisse Global Investment Returns Yearbook* p23
London Business School

DIVERSIFICATION: THE FOLLY OF CHASING RAPID GROWTH OVERSEAS

For those talking the loudest in the pub, the answers are simple. When it comes to choosing areas for great returns, then emerging markets[1] are the obvious place. The arguments are so straightforward that even the landlord's dog knows them. Emerging and frontier economies[2] could be giants when compared to the UK. They cover 46 per cent of the globe, and are home to more than five times the population of all the developed markets. But the killer argument is always on GDP. In simple terms, emerging and frontier markets offer the prospect of investing in dynamic economies growing faster than economies in the developed world.

Although these economies currently generate a smaller proportion of global wealth than mature markets, it's generally anticipated that this fast growth trend will continue. With the credit boom, investors have noted that the rate of expansion achieved by some of these economies has been quite exceptional. Rapid growth is anticipated to pay investors in faster capital gain. If fast growth is good, surely the fastest growth must be the best? It's worth investigating what these assumptions mean for asset allocation, and how these markets really fit with the Slow investment philosophy.

Institutional asset allocation into rapid growth equities for diversification

UK pension funds have been archetypal Slow investors. Compared with most others, they have the advantage of being able to take a truly long-term perspective. Although many have recently closed to new members, or

---

1 Emerging market: International Finance Corporation (IFC) definition refers to middle-to-higher income developing countries in transition to developed status. These economies were often undergoing rapid growth and industrialization, with stock markets that were increasing in size, activity and quality.

2 Frontier economy: Used by Standard & Poor's to denote pre-emerging economy

new contributions, they will continue to accrue return for many decades yet. With their Slow strategy, pension funds have traditionally believed it was appropriate to have the dominant portion of their assets in UK equities and UK bonds. Given that the liabilities of the UK pension schemes are principally in pounds, investing capital overseas clearly takes additional risks regarding overseas currency depreciation. But as the credit boom developed, questions were asked regarding their heavy reliance on the UK. Perhaps there would be greater benefits from investing in fast developing markets overseas.

According to data from WM,[3] the leading actuary to UK pension funds, asset allocation to the UK remained fairly stable, around 59-66 per cent for bonds and equities, during the early stages of the credit boom between 1985 and 1999. After that point, allocation into overseas equities and bonds progressively increased, doubling in just over a decade to 2006. Asian and other emerging equity markets were significant beneficiaries, with allocation increasing four-fold in the period. This capital flow fuelled the rapid expansion of the stock markets of the emerging countries, enhancing industrial capacity for these countries to export. Meanwhile asset allocation to the UK declined from around two thirds of the pension fund assets, to just 37 per cent by 2006. The attractions of participating in the globalisation trend seemed more compelling as it appeared that the trend was here to stay.

Not all of the capital invested overseas has gone to the high growth economies. One of the main beneficiaries of an increased capital allocation overseas has been the US, which after all has the largest equity and bond markets in the world. The percentage in US equities was not separately recorded prior to 1990, but its allocation has almost doubled in the twenty years to 2010. The financial sector is another major beneficiary; Hedge funds and Private Equity funds have been big winners in terms of allocation since 1999. From receiving almost negligible capital amounts just ten years ago, by 2010 together they amounted to 7 per cent of pension fund assets. The magnitude of these changes in just one decade is quite exceptional.

In contrast, allocations to other international markets including Europe[4] and Japan have remained strangely unaffected by the major shift towards international markets and more sophisticated financial products.

---

3   WM All Funds Universe, State Street Investment Analytics Asset Allocation 1985-2009
4   With the exception of the reduction in allocation to the UK

Fig 6.1: Asset allocation changes by UK pension funds
1985-2009

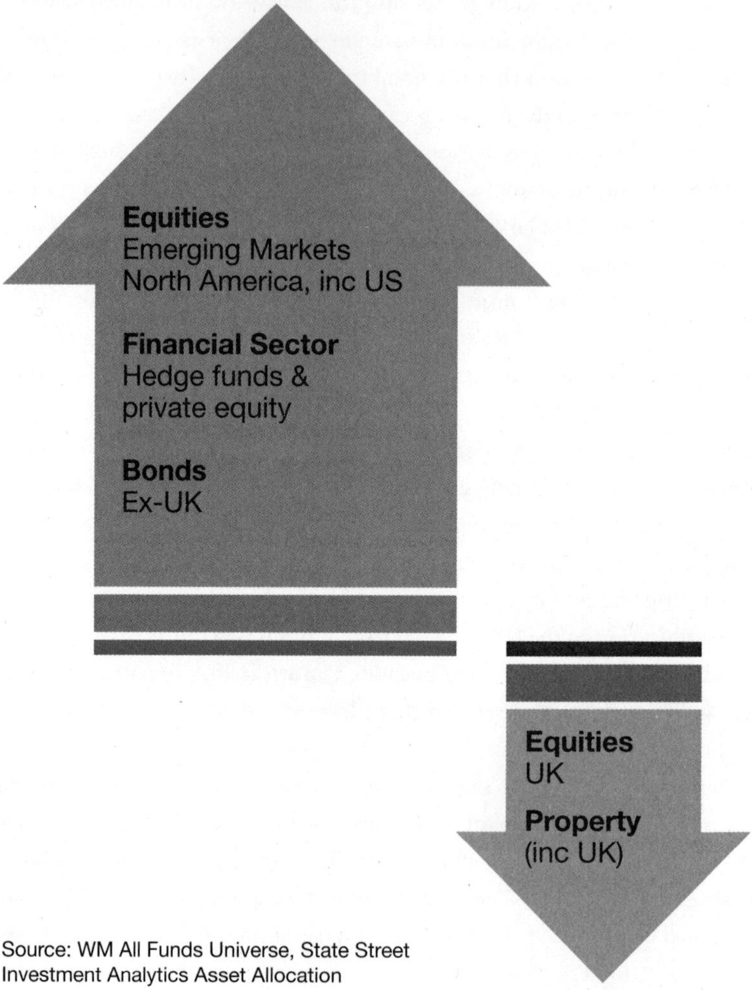

Equities
Emerging Markets
North America, inc US

Financial Sector
Hedge funds &
private equity

Bonds
Ex-UK

Equities
UK

Property
(inc UK)

Source: WM All Funds Universe, State Street
Investment Analytics Asset Allocation

Globalisation has been seen as inevitable. On the whole, the rationale behind the allocation change is that high growth economies offer scope for enhanced performance for investors, as well as lower risks through diversification benefits. For Slow investors taking the broad view, there are also questions to ask about whether Fast assumptions will remain valid if and when the credit boom comes to an end.

The development trajectory

Many developing countries are now assumed to be well on the way to becoming fully fledged developed nations, helped by an inflow of foreign capital. The underlying principle is relatively straightforward. Poor countries are deficient in capital relative to developed nations; that accounts for why they are poor after all. Classical economic theory suggests that countries with excess labour but deficient capital should offer excellent returns on any capital invested, and therefore should attract capital from developed nations.

But aside from the last couple of decades, things just haven't seemed to work that way. Capital flows have been extremely variable, subject to changes in sentiment, and the dominant flow has been from poor to rich. It has become apparent that access to capital is simply not enough for an emerging nation to successfully become a developed nation. In fact, over the last century, very few countries indeed have been able to make the transition from emerging to developed status.[5] They have included Japan, Finland, Portugal, Greece, Singapore and Taiwan; and in 2011, South Korea joined the list. But this list is very short given that so many countries aspire to make the change.

The highly regarded economist John Kay outlines what I believe is the most convincing reason to explain why emerging economies struggle to become developed nations. The critical feature appears to be the development of co-operative behaviour within their economies.[6] Although traditional societies have their own complex social rules, it is difficult for shared attitudes and behaviours to become established and embedded in the social and cultural institutions *of a nation*. As outlined in Chapter 2, investment flows must be considered in the context of the local values and customs of the recipient country.

Even though the rules of classical economics suggest all individuals make choices on what is best for them, in John Kay's view, an excessive emphasis on a 'me-first' culture works against the interests of the wider society. It inhibits the development of systems and institutions that help foster the right climate for investment capital. Most importantly, the suppliers of capital inflows need to be confident that if they take successively

---

5   Dimson, E, Marsh, P, Stauton, M (2010) *Credit Suisse Global Investment Returns Yearbook* p. 6 London Business School

6   Kay, J (2003) *The Truth about Markets: Why Some Nations Are Rich But Most Remain Poor*, Penguin, p. 338

greater risks, they won't be subject to too many unexpected or unfair restraints on their returns. It takes decades for norms to develop where the wider public recognises that it is good for everyone to work within established rules set out by institutions. Developing national institutions that ensure level playing fields is not something that happens quickly. The institutions that foster wealth creation, including financial institutions and regulatory systems,[7] are difficult to put in place, and without them it is difficult to build a market economy that can become developed and rich. Even though the rules of economics are broadly universal, investment capital will not flow consistently without local values and customs that are consistently supportive too. Essentially it is a slow process for a developing country to become a developed country in normal times.

> *'...the reason that poor countries, where unrestrained capitalism is practised, have not grown to become rich countries is that the whole process of building a successful economy in the longer term is related to development of ... co-operative institutions.'*

John Kay, The Truth about Markets[8]

Confidence in the stability and security offered by state-run institutions in developed nations – by the rule of law, by citizens knowing that they do not need to check and recheck the credentials of individuals working within the establishment – are exactly the reasons why capital often flows in a counter-intuitive direction, from poor to rich.[9] And it can be seen by the influx of foreign buyers into the London property market, for example. Their investment decisions are made in the confidence that their title is secure; they do not expect hasty legislative U-turns and so on. These are problems that act as constraints on economies that are still evolving and in a transition phase.

Nevertheless during the credit boom capital has been increasingly allocated to the fast growing emerging markets. Meanwhile analysis of returns from these markets throws up some surprising conclusions.[10] It

---

7   International Monetary Fund (2007) *Capital Flows speed catch-up in Europe* IMF Survey 13.06.2007

8   Kay, J (2003) *The Truth about Markets: Why Some Nations Are Rich But Most Remain Poor* Penguin

9   Lucas, R *Why Doesn't Capital Flow from Rich to Poor Countries?* American Economic Review 80 (2) pp. 92-96

10 Dimson, E, Marsh, P, Stauton, M (2010) *Credit Suisse Global Investment Returns Yearbook* p. 13 London Business School

suggests that the link between the rate of economic growth and the return on the relevant stock market is not straightforward.[11] Between 1985 and 2009, the Chinese economy grew at an astonishing average rate of 9.9 per cent per year. And yet the average return on the stock market was only 2.6 per cent per year. Germany was the slowest growing of the major economies for most of that period, following the economic indigestion caused by the reunification of East Germany. And yet the German stock market produced an average return of 6.1 per cent per annum in the same time period. The link between the rate of return on an equity market and the rate of growth of GDP is not as simple as is often assumed.

To complicate matters further, there *are* examples where high-growth economies that have delivered high stock market returns. A good example is India, which has grown at an annualised rate of 6.2 per cent between 1985 and 2009, delivering a very attractive annualised stock market return of 11.2 per cent per annum.

Fig 6.2: Annualised real GDP growth and equity returns 1985-2009

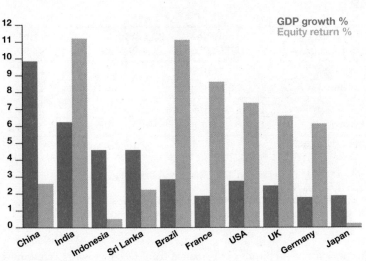

Source: Credit Suisse Global Yearbook 2010
Copyright © 2010 Elroy Dimson, Paul Marsh and Mike Staunton

---

11 Dimson, E, Marsh, P, Stauton, M (2010) *Credit Suisse Global Investment Returns Yearbook* p. 13 London Business School

Once again, it is worth emphasising that for most of the period of the study, the credit boom has been in place. If anything, the inclination of investors to buy the growth story rather than going for compounding dividend income will have enhanced returns from high growth economies. Over the ten years to 2010, many emerging stock exchanges have outperformed western markets. But history suggests that this strategy has not been particularly successful over longer time periods.

> *'...the absence of a clear-cut relationship between economic growth and stock returns should give investors pause for thought.'*[12]
> **Profs Elroy Dimson, Paul Marsh and Mike Staunton,**
> London Business School

The bottom line is that returns from slower growing, more mature economies as a group have often matched or indeed exceeded the stock market returns from the group of rapid growth economies since 1975!

Fig 6.3: Equity returns on markets ranked by past GDP growth

GDP ranked by 5 year past growth	19 countries 1900-2009	83 countries 1900-2009*	83 countries 1972-2009*
Lowest growth	10.9	14.1	25.1
Lower growth	9.3	11.7	18.6
Middling growth	10.1	10.6	16.2
Higher growth	7.8	9.0	11.9
Highest growth	11.1	13.1	18.4

Copyright © 2011 Elroy Dimson, Paul Marsh and Mike Staunton
London Business School
Source: Credit Suisse Global Investment Returns Yearbook
(*GDP data commencing as close as possible to 1900 or to 1972)

The absence of premium performance from faster growing economies could be explained by the fact that the behavioural bias towards overpaying for individual growth companies also applies to fast growth economies. Investing in stock markets with high expectations may have been

---

12 Dimson, E, Marsh, P, Staunton, M (2010) *Credit Suisse Global Investment Returns Yearbook* p. 17
London Business School

problematic because these expectations are already baked in the price. The professors of the London Business School believe this is the primary cause, 'Buying growth markets fails to outperform because markets anticipate economic growth.'[13] Greatest outperformance has come, in fact, from investing in economies showing signs of weakness.

In spite of this outcome, it is easy to understand why many emerging markets have seen attractive inflows of capital during the credit boom. The case as to whether the emerging nations have made the transition toward developed status may be uncertain. But capital has been plentiful during the credit boom and their growth rates have been just too large to ignore. Many assume the previous growth trends will continue. In thirty years, the total market capitalisation of emerging stock markets has increased six fold. If current trends continue, they could reach 30 to 50 per cent of the world total by 2050.[14] But the key message of *Slow Finance* is that the investment habits established during the credit boom should be treated with suspicion. With the credit boom coming to an end, all capital allocations will be under review. To what degree will 'Fast' investors sustain investment allocations to stock markets like China after the credit boom comes to an end?

China, the fast growth economy of the world

Many financial commentators expect the overall scale of the entire Chinese economy to overtake the overall scale of the US economy by the year 2020, so that it becomes the largest economy in the world.[15] In spite of the credit boom, China did not begin its 'Great Catch Up' until relatively late. Its major growth phase did not take off until the late 2000s. The attractions of investing in China's stock market are similar to other emerging countries and based upon the assumption that the rapid growth trends in their economy will offer great share price appreciation.

But in the case of China, the motivation for building a market economy with rapid economic growth is built upon socialist principles. The authorities in China are seeking economic expansion for reasons other

---

13 Dimson, E, Marsh, P, Stauton, M (2010) *Credit Suisse Global Investment Returns Yearbook* p. 17 London Business School

14 Dimson, E, Marsh, P, Stauton, M (2010) *Credit Suisse Global Investment Returns Yearbook* p. 7 London Business School

15 As China's population is approximately three times higher than that of the US, Gross Domestic Product (GDP) per capita basis would still be only one-third that of the equivalent figure in the US.

than the profit optimisation of their economy. In a research note published in 2011,[16] Andrew Hunt questioned to what degree China's rapid GDP growth was attributable to the conventional view based on the success of its export sector. Instead, he highlighted the impact of the internally driven, local-government led construction boom, funded by credit. Major infrastructure projects and even whole cities have been built despite the fact that many are barely being utilised.[17] This trend backs his view that, whilst recent investment has created genuine demand for commodities and labour, it may not be as productive as anticipated by external investors.

> *'...there is a significant probability that, through a mixture of over-enthusiasm, lack of fiscal discipline and straightforward graft, some of these projects were not warranted... if many of the assets turn out to be redundant, ill-sited or wasteful, we doubt that they will have added much to China's real long term prosperity. Instead, some of these assets could simply be China's "sub-prime" problem of property-related speculation and expenditure that was not really useful and which was financed by debts that may never be serviced let alone repaid.'[18]*

Andrew Hunt, Andrew Hunt Economics

Therefore the underlying profitability of the Chinese nation may be more marginal than most recognise.[19] Andrew Hunt's report highlights that overall profitability has been largely unchanged or declining in China, relative to the US, between 2007 and 2010. Rapid wage inflation has been especially damaging in this regard. Whilst the authorities may recognise the risks associated with wage inflation, the political cost of reining in the unproductive spending has been just too high.

To some degree economies can be likened to large businesses. During expansion phases there is a need for additional capital to fund the cost of adding new capacity; additional factories and such like. They also need to pay for the raw materials before they receive payment for the finished products that are ultimately sold. Capital inflows are entirely normal during rapid growth phases, even for companies or economies that are

---

16 Hunt, A (2011) *China: A Public Sector Boom* Andrew Hunt Economics 03.02.2011

17 Wall Street Journal 12.05.2010 *Revisiting China's empty city of Ordos* Merrill Lynch economist Ting Lu

18 Hunt, A (2011) *China: A Public Sector Boom* Andrew Hunt Economics 03.02.2011

19 I first worked with Andew Hunt in 1990. He has long-term experience following Asian emerging markets, living in Hong Kong for a many years.

generating good levels of profit. In the case of China, the multi-year period of very fast growth has led to sizable capital inflows from portfolio investors. Even though its stock markets are heavily restricted regarding its ownership by overseas investors, large amounts of western capital has found its way into their economy in one way or another. In addition many multinational companies have also invested heavily in new operations in China directly. China, as a nation, has enjoyed sizable capital inflows to fund the rapid growth of their economy, and still had plenty left over. This is the source of their huge capital surplus, which has been used to fund the sizable increase of borrowing by the developed economies. The low profitability of China has not been a significant issue, given that cash surpluses from the investment flows have funded the growth during the credit boom.

Abrupt changes in investor inclination to buy or sell are seen on an almost daily basis for individual quoted companies. Those with a long history of rising share prices can suddenly fall out of favour, as they go into a period of retrenchment. As businesses mature they are expected to increase dividends to sustain their attractiveness to investors given other investment alternatives. This is where the issue of underlying profitability becomes of critical importance. If the underlying business, or in the case of China, the underlying economy, has limited profitability, then it is constrained in its ability to pay out attractive levels of dividend income. Companies that don't generate decent cash flow suffer the greatest share price falls at times of disappointment since they don't have an offsetting dividend to bring in new buyers. The invisible hand of the market decides quite how much.

The professors at the London Business School have carried out some fascinating work investigating the advantage or otherwise of dividend income when investing in different stock markets. Professors Dimson, Marsh and Staunton compared the nineteen country stock markets where they have the data series for the last 111 years.[20] At the start of each year, they categorised those nineteen world stock markets into five groups according to the underlying yield on their indices. It was found that the markets with the highest yields outperformed those with lower yields,[21] matching the pattern found at stock level. But the big surprise was the differential

---

20 Dimson, E, Marsh, P, Stauton, M (2010) *Credit Suisse Global Investment Returns Yearbook* p. 18

21 Dimson, E, Marsh, P, Stauton, M (2010) *Credit Suisse Global Investment Returns Yearbook* p. 21

between the highest and lowest yielding exchanges. The annualised investment return on the stock markets with the lowest dividend yield each year was only 5.5 per cent. In comparison, those that were the highest yielding delivered an annualised return of 13.4 per cent.[22] A differential of 7.9 per cent per annum is simply extraordinary in the investment world.

- $1 invested in the highest yielding countries in 1900 compounded to a value of $1,000,000 by the end of 2010.[23]
- $1 invested in the low-yielders grew to a notional value of $370 in the same time period.

The results are persistent during the whole of the 111-year period, with each block of twenty-five years in the last century producing consistent results.

Fig 6.4: Returns from selecting world stock markets by yield 1900-2010

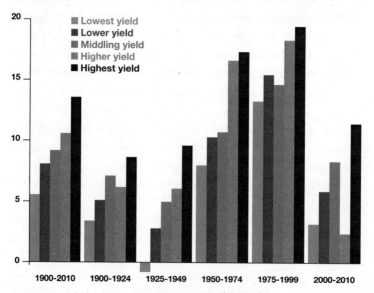

Source: Credit Suisse Global Investment Returns Yearbook 2011
Copyright © 2011 Elroy Dimson, Paul Marsh and Mike Staunton

---

22 These calculations take no account of tax or transaction costs

23 Dimson, E, Marsh, P, Stauton, M (2011) *Credit Suisse Global Investment Returns Yearbook* p. 21 London Business School

These results are very significant indeed for the Slow Investor. As with the individual stocks, it pays to compound returns over time through good and growing dividend income, not chase quick capital gains in very fast growth economies. This data suggests that following the end of the credit boom, the scale or otherwise of the dividend yield will be a major factor sustaining investor allocations. Perhaps a developed nation is one which can sustain a good flow of dividends even at times of economic difficulty. For investors, attractive stock markets will revert back to being those that have good and growing levels of dividend yield. Clearly this could have an effect on how investors perceive prospects for companies listed in countries like the UK. The analysis above suggests that underlying cash generated by the Chinese economy may not be enough to sustain a good dividend yield.

The implications of chasing Fast international growth

One of the problems with adopting a strategy that chases Fast growth is that as an asset appreciates, the appreciation itself often attracts a wider universe of potential investors. Is there a new story? How far might the asset price go? These attitudes may explain why the share prices of growth investments tend to over-shoot. In some ways it can be said that growth investors tend to be mean averse. Growth investors are more interested in buying a new investment if the share price is moving towards a new high rather than a new low. Their actions tend to be self-reinforcing, and therefore capital from these sources can build up to very sizable amounts.

I talked about Punch Group earlier as an example of a growth stock. In its case, the business used debt to enhance the rate of return on equity. With investor support it was able to grow rapidly through a series of sizable acquisitions, where the use of plentiful debt enhanced the returns for shareholders during the appreciating trend. However, since only a very small part of the investors' return came from accumulated dividends, almost all of the return was reliant upon the value of the share price. So in adverse times the sizable debt not only increased the vulnerability of a business, but also nearly all of their shareholders sought to exit since they stood to lose their entire return if they didn't sell quickly.

This kind of enhanced stop-start investor volatility is not too good on an individual stock basis. But with the credit boom, and the widespread adoption of growth investment strategies, whole countries have come under the same kind of pressures. For example, as the credit boom gained increased momentum in the mid-1990s, many of the smaller Asian countries found themselves swamped with growth capital looking to participate. Whilst it may appear to be a good thing at the time, excessive capital tends to erode the competitiveness of the underlying economy progressively. But when the upward momentum is lost, the capital quickly departs in large volumes, destabilising the capital base of the nation. Through this process, large amounts of growth capital pour in, dispensing apparent prosperity, but then often sluices out, causing poverty later. So with the Asian downswing in the late 1990s, many nations became impoverished almost overnight. In Thailand in 1998, the reversal in fortunes was so severe that the Finance Minister called for donations from the public to bolster the country's foreign currency reserves.[24] Thais were persuaded to offer their gold jewellery and even, allegedly, their gold teeth, in an attempt to bolster reserves to offset the devastating effects of the rapid withdrawal of investment capital. Although not quite so extreme, other examples of the scale and volatility of these changes in sentiment can be found in the peripheral nations of the Euro area in Greece, Ireland and Portugal in the middle of 2011. These effects are not just theoretical. They are real. They cause real hardship, since those who take on large debts to buy a home at the wrong time can find their lives blighted for years.

During the twenty-five years to 2011, the natural balance of Growth and Value Investors has been heavily skewed towards those favouring growth. Value Investors have often seemed out of touch and rather flat-footed by comparison. The Slow Investor has a lot in common with the Value Investor. Investing aggressively overseas for rapid growth is not a sustainable strategy. Whilst it might appear initially helpful, it is a strategy that tends to upset the slow process of becoming a developed nation. If anything, the experience of many of the fast growth nations reinforces the need for Slow Investors to be really sure to comprehend the impact that their capital is having on the ultimate recipients of their capital. Slow Investors can be much more effective in this task if they are close to their capital. There are plenty of quoted businesses with UK management teams that operate in international markets. Slow Investors can take advantage of the international diversification benefits of their capital by investing in

---

24 Crampton, C (1998) *Government to Ask for Donations of Gold Jewelry : Self-Help Glitters in Thailand* New York Times 02.01.1998

domestic businesses with overseas operations. They can monitor their investments easily, they have good access to the management teams, and they retain a close connection with their capital.

Slow Finance therefore proposes the introduction of **Investment Miles**, a new concept that highlights the gap between the investor and the proximity and nature of their ultimate investment. Investment Miles seek to measure the connectedness or otherwise of the investor and the business in receipt of the investor's capital. In the mind of a Slow Investor, a closer link between the investor and the investment is a win-win situation. Not only are the returns in the domestic businesses broadly as good as investing overseas, there are many other advantages of investing locally. Local risks are better known and understood, investor protection is more deeply rooted in the UK than many overseas locations, and the investment could have the potential positive spin-off benefits. It might stimulate domestic growth and create employment. In this way, Slow may give an extra impetus to the domestic economy.

'Slow Finance is the engine for sustained economic growth and job creation. A vibrant small and mid-cap sector is the UK's best opportunity for creating and maintaining sustainable growth, creating attractive returns for investors.'
Tim Ward, Chief Executive, UK Quoted Companies Alliance

It is important to keep the concept of Investment Miles simple. Therefore Investment Miles are calculated from just three components: the distance between the investment and the investor, the scale of the company and the number of employees that may be affected by the investment. The simple thesis is that the shorter the distance between the investment capital and the investor, the greater its influence as a shareholder. It is hoped that with a local connection there will be greater scope for the investor to act as an enlightened owner, in the style that Graham envisaged. This effect can be seen in the food arena; influence is greatest when the destination of consumer spend is closest to home. Directing food expenditure to those nearby boosts local economic activity and employment.

Investment Miles offer scope for Slow Investors to monitor more closely how well their investments are meeting the ideals set out in Slow Principles. Increasing the inclination to allocate capital locally would help in meeting these priorities. And typically, very small quoted companies find that investment capital can be very difficult to access, compared with larger international businesses. Investment Miles have a stronger bias to the smaller quoted businesses where the benefits of the increased investment allocation will be the greatest. Investment Miles also aim to deliver benefits to the greatest number of individuals.

Investment Miles are calculated by taking the number of miles between the investor and the investment, multiplied by the ratio of market capitalisation divided by number of employees.

Fig 6.5: Calculating investment miles

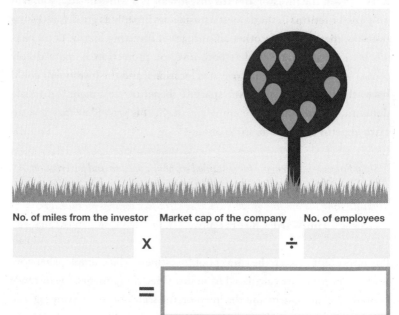

No. of miles from the investor   Market cap of the company   No. of employees

X   ÷

=

Copyright © 2011 Gervais Williams

In a similar manner to Food Miles, the ideal Investment Miles score is a small number. So if the company has a large number of employees and is smallish in terms of market capitalisation, then the term will be smaller than that of a very small company with very few employees. Conversely, it will be greater in scale for a large capitalisation business which employs very few staff, although if it was very close to the investor it would still not carry a large Investment Miles score. In the same way that Fair Miles are used in the food industry to measure rather more than just the geographical distance, the concept of Investment Miles also adds a little more insight from the investor's perspective. To some extent it reflects the scope for the Slow Investor to exercise a degree of influence in how the investment is directed, and through this process ensure that the Slow principles are supported.

Clearly Investment Miles should not be the sole measure for investment decision making for the Slow Investor. There are good reasons to diversify across a number of different industry sectors within a portfolio even if they do not all have low Investment Mile scores for example. And there *are* advantages to holding overseas assets, providing the Slow Investor is entirely clear why they are being held. Research suggests that investing in other economies is particularly advantageous when investing in stock markets that have premium levels of dividend income.

But there is a key drawback to investing overseas, and that is related to the size of the individual companies. If investment is contemplated in a business nearby, then investing in the full range of sizes of companies is a practical possibility. When investing overseas, it is difficult to invest with confidence in the very smallest companies, as they are difficult to manage from the UK. In addition, since they are small they are illiquid, so it can be difficult to invest or disinvest at will. Think carefully. Investing directly in tiny quoted businesses far from home is probably a risk too far.

Through sluicing large amounts of investment capital into and out of fast growing emerging economies, we not only cause potential imbalances in those countries' development, but also may impede the development of the co-operative institutions that are essential for them to gain developed status. Successful Slow investing is not about quick turnarounds and short-term gains. Using Investment Miles, Slow Investors can begin to make investments that support not only local and national growth but which also encourage a more responsible attitude towards spreading their capital overseas.

THINKING SMALL: BIG STOCKS DON'T ALWAYS MEAN BIG RETURNS

If you look at almost any professional portfolio of equities, most of the capital will be invested in businesses that are amongst the largest quoted on the relevant stock market. There are a number of practical advantages that institutions enjoy when holding larger companies in their portfolios. The question for Slow Investors, of course, is whether large companies should also be the focus for them. Put simply: is bigger really better for those seeking to adopt the Slow principles?

There are a number of reasons why a larger company investment might be favoured. Firstly, because companies are large, it is the case that they are typically more resilient than the tiddlers. Big companies are often better known, and have strong brands that sustain sales of their services or products more consistently throughout the economic cycle. They are normally relatively robust and well spread in terms of their customer base. As a result, few larger companies go into receivership, even during recessions, and so are often well positioned to benefit when the economy recovers.

Large businesses also have access to a wider range of sources of funding for operations. This is one of their strongest advantages. Lack of access to finance is one of the most common reasons why it is difficult to grow a smaller business. In contrast, larger companies are considered attractive borrowers for the banks and the corporate bond market. If larger businesses are more resilient, there is a greater chance that they will be able to service their debt even at times of difficulty, which makes them better prospects for lending than smaller companies. This feature is particularly true for large companies that are listed on a stock exchange. Even when these companies do get caught out with excessive debt at a time when the economy suddenly enters a recession, then they can normally survive by resorting to a stock market fundraising. Whilst it is almost inevitable that the share price of such a business may fall back sharply, the management team can usually arrange a secondary issue to repay part of the debt and thereby stabilise the business. It will then be secure until demand in the economy starts to recover.

A particularly good example of a quoted company using a share issue to refinance the business after an unexpected setback was Barratt Developments plc after the 2008 financial crisis. Barratt is the biggest house builder in the UK, normally selling over 10,000 houses each year. During the years up to 2007, it was growing rapidly, selling more houses each year. However, when the banking crisis arrived in 2008, not only did homebuyers become more nervous about making large financial commitments, but many banks were also constrained in their ability to fund most mortgage applications. Barratt and all the other house builders suddenly found they had spent capital on building new homes ready for sale, but had comparatively few buyers. With the lack of sales, not only did the company slip into loss, but its debt burden was also uncomfortably large. However, being a larger quoted business meant that Barratt was able to issue new shares to raise additional capital. In contrast, most unquoted house builders were unable to raise additional capital and may have risked receivership as a result.

Thirdly, institutions often favour large quoted businesses because they are liquid. An institutional fund manager with a sizable amount of capital to invest finds that larger quoted companies are well suited to their needs. The largest companies have a larger number of shareholders; throughout the opening hours of the stock market there is active trading of their shares. So for the active institutional fund manager, this presents an opportunity to adjust the amount of capital invested in the company at a time of their choosing. This is often most useful when unexpected events occur. For example, when the banking crisis hit in 2008, institutional shareholders were able to adjust the amount of capital they had allocated to house builders, as they may have anticipated that the availability of mortgages would fall sharply. Liquidity, as it is known, or the ability to increase or decrease an institutional shareholding is regarded as particularly important. Large companies are liquid.

To summarise, holding larger companies have several key advantages. They are perceived as less vulnerable to unexpected events, they may have greater resilience due to their ability to raise additional capital if required and it is relatively easy for fund managers to change their allocation to individual stocks at will. These features seem to imply that non-professional investors should follow the trend of the institutions and concentrate on companies of larger size, to insulate themselves from the worst effects of downturns and position themselves for the long-term. This is not altogether correct. The greater use of debt by larger companies, the costs of managing organisations of very large size, and the productivity and historic stock market data all point in the *opposite* direction. Part of the investment future, it appears, could be with smaller companies; an outcome that could be a win-win for Slow Investors seeking to re-engage with their investments on a more human scale.

Large companies and correlation with world economic growth

Institutions invest their clients' capital in the hope of delivering returns that are perhaps a little ahead of those of the overall stock market. In doing so, a pension fund for example aims to accumulate sufficient capital to more than cover all of the client pensions. Although the stock market has been volatile since the millennium, the overall rate of return for investors has generally been reasonably positive. WM Company acts as an adviser to a very large percentage of the pension fund assets in the UK.[1] Despite the financial crisis in 2008, in the five years to 2009[2] the average pension fund has made an annualised return of 5.2 per cent.[3] Over the longer term WM clients have averaged a return of 9.4 per cent over the twenty-five years to 2009.[4] This is good news for pension funds as it is usefully above the rate of increase in average wages, and therefore the capital fund has grown faster than the pension requirements of its members. The 9.4 per cent return is also well above the annualised rate of inflation in the period. However, these returns were made in the period of the credit boom when the rates of return on equities were unusually good. During the credit boom, nearly all asset prices have moved up more rapidly than the long term trend. This has been particularly true for medium and larger businesses where pension funds tend to have their biggest holdings.

One of the key questions is how much of that strong stock market performance by larger companies can be attributed to their superior market position, and how much is down to the buoyant credit-fuelled environment before 2007. The US bank Citibank carried out research in 2008 to try to

---

1   End 2010: WM acted as advisor to £444 bn of UK pension assets, mainly invested in equities

2   To 2010

3   WM All Funds Universe, State Street Investment Analytics 2011

4   WM All Funds Universe, State Street Investment Analytics 2011

identify the key reasons for their strong performance during the previous decades, and to establish how much the growth of the world economy contributed to the returns of larger businesses.[5] It concluded that, on average, 71 per cent of the return was explained by the rate of growth of the world economy. Just 29 per cent of the return of an individual larger business is explained by factors that are specific to the company itself.

In many ways this conclusion is not unexpected. Large quoted companies tend to have international operations. Their progress, or the lack of it, is likely to be correlated to the general overall trend of economic expansion. This is a blessing in good economic periods as the rising economic tide is likely to float all larger company ships. Nearly all larger businesses would be expected to participate in the general expansion, since as a group they have a large market share of many of these expanding markets. However, in times of world recession, the boot is very much on the other foot. Larger businesses find it hard to dodge the bullets because they have major market positions, at a time when activity levels are falling.

Now that the credit boom is coming to an end, and once central banks cease to expand quantitative easing, it can be anticipated that credit demand is likely to grow at a much slower pace. Indeed, it is logical that credit demand may actually grow slowly for an extended period, as those parts of the economy that are overextended in terms of debt will either repay borrowings or, at the very least, hold back from increasing their current levels of borrowing. This is why most financial commentators believe that world economic growth is likely to be subnormal for an extended period. With such a close correlation between world economic growth and the performance of larger companies, it suggests that overall stock market indices which are dominated by large company shares could prove disappointing in terms of investment returns for many years.

Large companies still have substantial borrowings

While large companies have been able to borrow relatively cheaply over the last twenty-five years, they now face a difficult scenario. Many have used low cost debt as an opportunity for debt-funded expansion, but they face a slower growth future. The economist Andrew Hunt highlights that companies have generally not used the buoyant period of the stock market

---

5   *The law of large numbers* (2008) Citibank Investment Research & Analysis 30.06.08

after Quantitive Easing to repay much of the borrowings taken on during
the credit boom. This is despite the fact that many companies have enjoyed
record low interest rates on what they have borrowed both in the US and
the UK.[6] In my view, these large amounts of debt will be regarded amongst
investors as more problematic after the credit boom has come to an end.
Larger companies have often taken full advantage of the easy availability of
debt during the credit boom, and so may feel they want to cut back on
their debt burdens significantly in the future. This may constrain their
ability to pay increased dividends.

Fig 7.1: Have large companies borrowed too much?

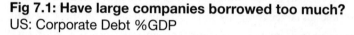

US: Corporate Debt %GDP

UK: Corporate Debt %GDP

Source: Andrew Hunt, Andrew Hunt Economics 2011

---

6   Hunt, A (2010) *Life on Mars?* Andrew Hunt Economics 14.04.2010

Big companies are complex

While the macro-economic environment is going to be challenging, there are also a number of internal reasons why larger businesses may find life difficult in the lean times. One is their complexity. It is possible to argue that, in a challenging world, big businesses need to be complex. Size incurs a need for more internal co-ordination. As scale develops, increasingly sophisticated administrative systems for providing management information have also developed to help the business address uncertainties. So, in one sense, size and complexity have come to be linked with progress. Greater specialisation is often regarded as a good thing; it often requires greater sophistication to achieve it, so in this regard, complexity is within a larger business by design.

However, there is another form of complexity too. That is one that becomes engrained in an organisation and remains in place even when the reasoning for the original process has long passed. Ron Ashkenas has written extensive literature on these issues for the Harvard Business Review.[7] He often includes anecdotes to highlight how unintentional complexity comes about:

> 'The president of a large company with several business units and staff functions asked his CFO to put together a weekly, nonfinancial "activity report" so that he would be up-to-date on key developments or changes in each part of the company. To produce this report, the CFO asked each of the business heads and functional directors to give him a few highlights each week from their areas. Most of these people then asked their subordinates to do the same, so the request cascaded down through several levels. As the information came back up each week it had to be aggregated and summarised and before long a number of people in various parts of the organisation were spending considerable time producing this report. The president of course was oblivious to the "information industry" that sprung up around the activity report, thinking that his request was simple and straightforward.'[8]
>
> **Ron Ashkenas**, Business Commentator

---

7   Ashkenas, R (2009) *Simply Effective: How to Cut Through Complexity in Your Organization and Get Things Done*, Harvard Business School Press 2009

8   Ashkenas, R (2010) Harvard Business Review Blog Network *Are you in cahoots with complexity?* Blogs.hbr.org/ashkenas/2010/08/are-you-in-with-comple:htm

Complexity of this type relates to the way that organisations evolve over time. In particular, merging large and complex businesses in itself often 'bakes in' established ways that things get done within the business. And this position can multiply when larger organisations join together. As Ron Ashkenas notes:

> *'Complexity is the cumulative by-product of organisational changes, big and small, that over the years weave complications (often invisibly) into the way work is done.'*[9]

> **Ron Ashkenas**, Business Commentator

Clearly, the senior management team of any business seeks to eliminate organisational inefficiencies. Inefficiencies impede the way a business responds to market change and client need. But despite management's best efforts, excessive complexity is endemic within very large organisations. Perhaps that is why large organisations rarely do great things. Excessive complexity leaves many employees too cut off from what is happening in the world around them, or hamstrung to act freely to bring new solutions to market.

Large organisations are often well equipped to deal with conventional difficulties. They have many experienced specialists within the company that can tackle conventional challenges. But they are poorly structured to deal with ambiguous problems; those that are characterised by questions about what is unknown. New methods, evolving technologies... these are areas where large organisations often fall short as they are unable to recognise them for what they are.[10] Large company complexity is relevant to investors as it means that large companies are rarely able to excel. Ultimately, many larger businesses decline, held back by the inertia of their processes, as internal inefficiencies overwhelm them and demand for their more constrained service levels fall away. Where are all the large railway and shipping companies that were so profitable 100 years ago?

---

9   Ashkenas, R (2007) Cited in Cunha, M.P (2008) *Complexity, simplicity, simplixity* University of Lisbon. Prepared for Organisational Studies Workshop, Cyprus 2008

10 Zeckhauser, R (2006) reprinted in 2010 in *The Known, the Unknown, and the Unknowable in Financial Risk Management: Measurement and Theory Advancing Practice*, eds Diebold, F, Doherty, N & Herring, R Princeton University Press. Examples cited include evolving medical technologies including neo-organ development

Of course, there are well-known exceptions to this rule. Dev Patnaik, Founder and CEO of Jump Associates, believes this is more related to what he calls hybrid thinking within the leadership of a business:

'Hybrid thinking... is about having multidisciplinary people – folks who are one-part humanist, one-part technologist and one-part capitalist. When multiple disciplines inhabit the same brain, something magical starts to happen. The disciplines themselves start to mutate. They hybridise. We start practicing business like a designer... We shape technology like a culturalist... And we start thinking about the most complex problems that plague our societies like an entrepreneur.'[11]

Dev Patnaik, CEO, Jump Associates

In Mr Patnaik's view, leaders of large companies, like Steve Jobs at Apple, for example, are not genius minds that show up only intermittently each generation. What makes them rare is that they lead larger companies. These are companies where hybrid eccentricities are tolerated, but it is unlikely that the same individual would be appointed to mature larger organisations where conventional management processes are the norm. Large organisations grind people down to become specialist cogs in their massive machines. Patnaik's thinking suggests that there is a limit where the scale of business and the implicit web of internal complexity *exceeds* the cost efficiencies gained from buying advantages and so on.

This theorem meshes well with the work of Mans Soderbom of the University of Gothenburg.[12] Soderbom carried out a comprehensive study, published in 2011, comparing the scale of business with the underlying efficiency of many companies, using a variety of different methods. The study used a comprehensive database based on 30,000 Swedish organisations between 1997 and 2006, and is extremely detailed. From the data, he was able to gain a good understanding of how efficiency changed with the size of the business as measured by their number of employees. He concluded that **the most efficient businesses had 250 employees or less**. In addition, these companies were often able to expand quickly if there was good demand for their products. But as firms exceeded 250

---

11 Patnaik, D (2011) *Why can't big companies solve big problems?* Fast Company for Jump Associates

12 Soderbom, M, Sato, Y (2011) *Are larger firms more productive due to scale economies? – A contrary evidence from Swedish microdata* University of Gothenburg

employees, then the scale benefits began to be more than offset by a reduction of internal efficiency. Many larger companies remained profitable, but there was evidence that growing internal inefficiencies progressively impeded them as they got larger.

Fig 7.2: Size and productivity
Can larger companies deliver?

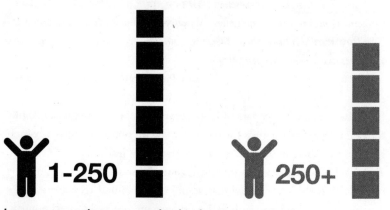

Larger companies are perceived to be more productive, but research shows this is not the case.

Analysis of 30,000 Swedish companies over ten years shows:
– Increasing productivity with scale:
   micro firms (less than 10 employees),
   small firms (10-50) and
   smaller-medium sized firms (50-250 employees)
– Decreasing productivity in larger firms with over 250 employees

Source: Soderbom, M. Sato, Y. (2011). *Are larger firms more productive due to scale economies? - A contrary evidence from Swedish microdata.* University of Gothenburg.

This data implies that investors may find that the investment risk/ reward ratio is most attractive outside the largest companies. It may be that smaller businesses are not only more efficient, and thus may generate more profit on their sales, but also have the best opportunities to grow rapidly. This is an important conclusion for any investor seeking premium returns in a world where overall investment returns may be modest.

Are smaller companies too small for institutional portfolios?

Ask any major institutional investor anywhere in the world, and there is one factor that they all agree on: investing in small, micro-capitalisation companies is not worth the effort. Small businesses are fiddly. They are not the best route to participate in the globalisation trend. Worst still, from an institutional investment manager's point of view, smaller company investment requires a lot of staff to administer a small part of the overall portfolio.

The term 'blue-blooded' is often used to describe a person of royal descent. 'Blue chip' is a term given to certain stocks and denotes the identical connection in the stock family. Blue chips are regarded as the safest and best stocks investors can possibly own. They are regarded as solid, dependable stocks that will deliver good returns year after year to investors. A few obvious ones that come to mind in the UK are Weir, GlaxoSmithKline and Vodafone.

In the UK, the Alternative Investment Market (AIM) was set up to provide capital to the small and micro-cap businesses that offered rapid growth and generated additional employment. However, since it was first initiated in 1996, returns from some exciting upswings have been offset by some dark periods, including one at the peak of the credit crisis. Overall, since 1996, it has delivered a zero return to investors![13] But this conceals the fact that investors in this market tend not to focus on all the stocks represented in the benchmark FTSE AIM All Share index, but to concentrate on individual stock stories. However because the daily transactions in the small and micro-sectors are infrequent, it is hard for the institutional investor to invest or disinvest at will. Investment in small and micro-cap companies requires a commitment to investment on a long-term basis. Financial attitudes during the credit boom have favoured the ability to sell investments quickly. Institutions just don't want to make such a commitment, preferring to believe they can deal themselves out of trouble ahead of the crowd in the mid and large quoted companies.

In a world where unexpected events occur regularly, investors believe they have good reason to avoid the illiquid stocks in the small company universe. The sums that can be realistically invested in such companies are just too tiny relative to the very large sums they manage for their clients. Where institutional portfolios hold smaller companies, it's normally as a

---

13 FTSE AIM All Share Inception to 2010
   AIM: London's market for small and micro growing companies

result of a larger company producing disappointing returns, with a consequent collapse in share price, so that it becomes a small and micro-capital stock by default. In the institutional mind, smaller companies are linked with problems and failure.

Davies, Fama and French carried out additional analysis on Value investing.[14] Their work also calculated the historic performance of smaller businesses compared with larger companies. Using data from the New York Stock Exchange between 1929 and 1997, they calculated that the smaller company universe outperformed by 0.2 per cent on average per month. This compares with between 0.4 and 0.5 per cent per month outperformance for Value investments versus Growth investments covered in Chapter 4.[15]

Although these numbers appear small, they build up into very large numbers over time. So if smallcap stocks were to continue to outperform in the future by 0.2 per cent per month, then in one year they would have outperformed by 2.43 per cent, since in each month the added value from outperformance would compound in the same way as dividends compound. After five years, that rate of outperformance would total 12.74 per cent. And after fifteen years it would be 43.33 per cent. The compounding effect means that the five-year number is more than five times the one-year number, and the fifteen-year number is more than three times the five-year number. These are average figures of course, and the actual figures vary each year.

In addition, Davies, Fama and French also reviewed data which looked at both the Small Cap Effect and the Value Effect combined.[16] As might be expected, the best-performing strategy is that of the Smaller Value businesses, and the least successful strategy is the Larger Growth businesses. Over the period from 1929 to 1997, the Small Value group of companies averaged an absolute 1.53 per cent per month, whereas the Large Growth stocks averaged 0.89 per cent.

- $1 invested in an index portfolio of the Small Value universe would have grown to $24,044,586 by the end of 1997 (sixty-eight years is a very long period over which to invest!).

- $1 in the Large Growth portfolio would have grown to $137,956.

---

14 See Chapter 4 on Value investing

15 Davies, J.L, Fama, E.F, French, K.R (2000) *Characteristics, Covariances and Average Returns 1929-1997* Journal of Finance LV (1)

16 Davies, J.L, Fama, E.F, French, K.R (2000) *Characteristics, Covariances and Average Returns 1929-1997* Journal of Finance LV (1)

Remember that this data contains the period when Microsoft grew to become one of the largest companies in the period and would have been classified as a Large-Growth business for a large part of the study period.

This performance differential is **enormous**. While dealing costs have not been deducted from the calculations and large institutions will never be able to put a very large percentage of their assets into a Small-Cap Value strategy, with these kinds of differentials going begging, it does appear that some institutions are overlooking a decent investment strategy. Fortunately, this is not an impediment for Slow Investors. The key question for those interested in the Slow principles is whether a similar trend has been observed in the UK.

Hoare Govett has sponsored research on UK smaller companies by Dimson and Marsh of London Business School since 1987.[17] The details of the RBSHBC index were outlined in chapter 4, page 79. Their analysis of the size effect in the UK market offers a number of important conclusions.

Performance of smaller quoted businesses

Over the long-term, UK smaller companies have delivered greater investment returns than larger ones. Smaller businesses tend to grow faster than larger ones, and sometimes corporate bidders offer next year's share price today. In Chapter 4 it was noted that £1 invested in 1955 in the average UK small company would have grown to a capital sum of £218 in 2010 before dividends, or £3248 with income reinvested.[18] £1 invested in the FTSE All-Share Index would have grown to become £55 in the same period, or £620 with dividends reinvested.

This key finding is that investing in smaller companies in the UK offers premium performance just as it does in the US. In a similar manner to the US study, smaller companies have accumulated a return that is many multiples of that accumulated by larger companies. Although investing in the smallest companies is more awkward, the returns to investors are much more attractive. The annualised rate of return on the FTSE All-Share index was 12.2 per cent per annum, compared with 15.6 per cent for the RBS Hoare Govett Smaller Companies (RBS HGSC) index. Both of these numbers include the benefit of including the annual dividends in the calculation, as if this cash were used to purchase more shares each year.

---

17 See also observations on international v UK performance in Chapter 6

18 Dimson, E, Marsh, P (2011) RBS HGSC Annual Report (2011) *Index performance data* p. 22

Fig 7.3: The power of small
Cumulative value

2010
_____
RBS HG 1000

£7,393

RBS HGSC

£3,248

FTSE All-Share

£620

1955
_____
£1 Invested

Source: RBS HGSC Annual Report 2011
(Returns including capital gain with dividend income reinvested)

Most UK institutional funds find it difficult to deliver a return for their investors that exceeds the FTSE All-Share index. So an outperformance of 3.4 per cent each year would exceed the returns generated by almost every unitised or UK equity portion of a UK pension fund, even those that are at the top of the performance charts. Outperformance of this size is very significant because almost no investment funds are able to achieve it.

To identify the smaller small company effect, the professors divided all the companies in the RBS HGSC into two groups based on size. Dimson and Marsh also broke their universe into two groups: Value and Growth. To some extent what exactly constitutes 'Value' varies between investors. In a similar way to Davies, Fama and French, the professors did this by comparing the market capitalisation of the company with that of the underlying assets in the business. It is worth noting that in terms of the market capitalisation, there is scope for larger or smaller businesses to be within the Value or Growth definitions.

Following this classification, the companies in the HGSC fell into one of four groups:

1. **Larger Growth small cap**
2. **Smaller Growth small cap**
3. **Larger Value small cap**
4. **Smaller Value small cap**

The RBS HGSC consituents are reclassified every year, but there have been some distinctive longer-term performance trends. The Value universe of stocks has massively outperformed the Growth universe. The Value stocks produced cumulative returns that are 7.5 times greater than Growth stocks. When the bias for Smaller Small companies to outperform is included as well, then the premium return generated in the past has been very large indeed. The Small Value smaller company has compounded at a rate of 20.7 per cent over the last fifty-six years. Even the Larger Value smaller company has compound returns of 18.6 per cent. It is a very long time since 1955, but differentials of this magnitude over such a long period are simply **huge**. The FTSE All-Share index has compounded at 12.2 per cent over the same period.

Of course it is worth remembering also that the RBS HGSC indices are rebalanced at the start of each year and therefore an individual stock can find itself in different classifications at the beginning of different years. For example, if a stock is highly favoured by investors and the market capitalisation is well above the assets on its balance sheet, it may fall into the Growth classification. But if, say, a few years later, it has a period of slow growth and falls out of favour, then the share price could fall back enough for it to qualify for the Value designation. But the implications of these calculations are that Benjamin Graham of *The Intelligent Investor* really was on to something when he first articulated his Value approach to investing.[23] He was a Slow Investor ahead of his time.

The scale effect and the Slow Investor

For Benjamin Graham, there was little data available on the performance of the smaller company universe at the time he was writing his book, so he did not really address the issue of small capitalisation investment. Some believe he was only interested in larger companies but contrary to popular belief, Benjamin Graham was open-minded to investing in any business, providing the decision was based on sound rationale.

> *'Have the courage of your knowledge and experience. If you have formed a conclusion from the facts and if you know your judgment is sound, act on it – even though others may hesitate or differ. You are neither right nor wrong because the crowd disagrees with you. You are right because your data and reasoning are right.'*
>
> **Benjamin Graham**, *The Intelligent Investor*[24]

But for those interested in Slow investing, there does seem to be real merit in investing in smaller companies, in particular smaller small-cap companies. However, this strategy seems to work much better if it's combined with a similar bias favouring investments with intrinsic Value.

The Slow principles in Chapter 2 favoured investments that were relatively straightforward and easy to comprehend. They suggest investing in companies that are relatively small, and preferred companies that had demonstrable benefits for the local economy which may generate additional employment. In a slower-growth world, small businesses will have an important role to play in injecting some dynamism into the economy.

> *'The evidence all points towards small and medium-size enterprises being the core drivers of UK economic recovery. If we assume the three key challenges we face are addressing the trade balance, building a long-term replacement for our heavy manufacturing and strengthening employment, our innovative small businesses seem best equipped to deliver.'*
>
> **Marcus Stuttard**, Head of AIM

---

23 Graham, B (1986) *The Intelligent Investor* 4th edition, Harper & Row

24 Graham, B (1986) *The Intelligent Investor* 4th edition, Harper & Row

The Slow principles anticipate that investors will regain a greater interest in investing in individual companies, rather than just companies that are members of specific indices. It is entirely obvious that the Slow principles dovetail perfectly with the strategy of investing in smaller small companies with a Value bias. Those willing to anticipate and adopt the Slow investment principles can expect to reconnect more closely with the purpose of their investment, perhaps using Investment Miles to inform their decisions. Simply put, it is difficult for all investors to invest in smaller small companies anywhere other than relatively local to their location. In combination, the principles should help investors to be well-placed to gain relatively attractive returns when compared with most other investors in the UK stock market.

In the next chapter it will be seen that despite these very long-term trends, there are periods when the Large Growth companies perform better against the long-term trend. As highlighted earlier, there are real advantages in diversifying investments. Smaller companies have greater risks of becoming insolvent, are less resilient and are relatively illiquid. Therefore it would be unwise to have too large a portion of an individual portfolio in these assets, despite their outstanding long-term performance. There is a place for larger and mid-sized companies in portfolios, even for Slow Investors, in spite of academic research which suggests that internal complexity of larger businesses constrains their efficiency. By being large, these stocks have a good volume of daily transactions, and it's easy for investors to adjust their stock positions if needed, even at relatively short notice. Mid-sized and larger companies clearly offer diversification benefits. The key issue is to find a way of ensuring that the strategy for selecting stocks for that mid and large cap portfolio are also made on criteria which are compatible with the Slow principles. Beyond that, the optimal approach seems to involve combining the benefits of liquidity of mid-sized and larger companies with the key elements of the UK 'smaller company effect' and the Value bias.

In the next chapter we will draw together all the evidence outlined in the previous chapters, and note how these very long-term trends have been affected over the credit boom. We will also outline a specific method of how to identify Slow investments; those which tend to match Slow principles, and how these might be monitored in the UK. Slow Finance aims to assist Slow Investors in identifying the smaller small companies that may best meet their investment needs.

WHEN TO ACT: USING TIMING FOR INVESTMENT SUCCESS

The Slow Investor's goal is to develop an investment strategy that allows them to re-engage with their investments – to exert influence, and make meaningful choices about where and how their investment is put to work. *Slow Finance* suggests using rules of thumb to help do that, by narrowing the pool of potential investments to those with **smaller market capitalisations,** stocks that offer **value,** companies paying **good and growing dividends** and those that are **local.** The recipe has been explained but one essential ingredient is missing. Timing. Understanding when to act, and when to pause.

Benjamin Graham's solution meant working out formula timing plans to try to identify when to buy and when to sell stocks. 'I am more and more impressed with the possibilities of history's repeating itself on many different counts', he said. '... In recent years certain compromise methods have been devised by which the investor can take some advantage of the stock market's cycles without running the risk of an unduly long wait or of "missing the market" altogether.'[1]

This is where it gets interesting. Today, we have technology to make the process of monitoring investment performance easier. But in order to really understand risk and return, it is important to take the long view. On the stock market, 'unusual' or off-trend returns can last as long as ten or twenty years.[2] We cannot anticipate next year's events, but analysing very extensive data over very long time periods can help reveal what investment themes have worked in the past. Understanding the history gives us context, and that can help guide the timing of decisions.

---

1   Graham, B (1949) Cited by Barker, D (2010) *Benjamin Graham's Investing Wisdom and Formula Timing Plans* The Market Oracle 27.11.2010

2   Dimson, E, Marsh, P Stauton, M (2011) *Credit Suisse Global Investment Returns Yearbook* p. 7 London Business School

At the moment, some important features are coming together. We know that size and value are features that have a major effect on stock market returns. We know that over the last fifty-six years in the UK, smaller companies have outperformed the larger listed universe by an average of 3.4 per cent per year.[3] We also know that the smaller companies effect – where companies with lower market capitalisation tend to outperform larger ones – dissipated from 1988 as the credit boom took off. At the same time, we are experiencing the longest period on record when value within the smaller companies world monitored by the FTSE Small Cap Index has underperformed.[4] We also know that local investors can enjoy a performance edge over distant rivals,[5] and that the compounding effect of companies making generous dividend distributions can be powerful.[6]

Not all of the Slow strategies are flavour of the moment, but this is a moment of flux. The challenge is to stand back, to be tenacious in seeking the facts and considered in taking action.

Why small fell out of favour

The smaller companies effect – which has been in the spotlight since the 1980s[7] – is well recognised in academic circles, but it seems to have fallen off the radar for many investors. In my view, the reason for this is clear. We have just experienced what could be one of the largest credit booms in history, and access to capital has had a distorting effect.

Credit booms favour businesses with easy access to cheap credit. Those with the greatest access can take greatest advantage of rising asset values by buying additional assets on credit to enhance their returns. Those who are unable to access credit easily cannot take advantage in the same way. Not all quoted companies have had easy access to borrowing, and there has been a marked difference between large and small companies in this regard. Typically, larger companies have had very good access to debt, at a cheaper rate than smaller businesses. The access of quoted small cap stocks to debt has been limited and become much worse since 2008. This

3   Dimson, E, Marsh, P *RBS HGSC Index Annual Report* (2011) p. 22 London Business School

4   Dimson, E, Marsh, P *RBS HGSC Index Annual Report* (2011) p. 6 London Business School

5   Malloy, C (2003) *The Geography of Equity Analysis* Harvard Business School, NBER

6   Dimson, E, Marsh, P Stauton, M (2011) *Credit Suisse Global Investment Returns Yearbook* p. 44 London Business School

7   Banz, R (1981) *The relationship between return and market value of common stocks* Journal of Financial Economics 9 pp. 13–18

differential has favoured the stock market performance of larger companies over the period of the credit boom. Indeed, over the last twenty-five years, the competition to supply credit became so intense that it encouraged the development of new methods of financing quoted companies, including the evolution of the corporate bond market.

Its evolution has not been helpful for smaller quoted companies. The scale of their borrowing tends to be much less extensive than that of larger companies. Since the cost of issuing a corporate bond is spread over the amount of debt issued, a smaller debt issue tends to carry higher costs. Not only that, but with a small amount of debt in issue, there's also much less daily trading of the debt in the secondary market. Institutional investors don't like this, as they find it more difficult to value their portfolios each evening and the smaller business is assumed to have a less stable profit profile. Investors in small corporate bond issues tend to need a much higher rate of interest to offset some of the negatives. And even if these issues get away, they are by their nature small so institutions can't get a meaningful amount of capital invested. So for the smallest quoted companies, the scope to issue corporate bonds to fund their business growth is reliant upon the interests of smaller investors and private client stockbrokers. Even for some not-so-small quoted companies, the banks would rather work on a larger bond issue from a bigger business where they can gain a higher total commission on a larger issue of corporate debt.

Smaller companies have lost out in accessing newer methods of lending, in spite of the overall boom in credit supply over the last twenty-five years. Indeed, if anything, there has been a decline in traditional corporate banking offering overdrafts, as the larger quoted companies have ditched this method in favour of using corporate bonds. With the drop in demand for overdrafts, banks have cut the number of staff in these departments and re-allocated them to the growing market for corporate bonds. Traditional corporate lending has been a sector in decline and, with the arrival of the credit crunch, there have been periods when the banks have declined to renew existing overdraft facilities for smaller quoted companies. Where the banks have found it politically embarrassing to refuse these, then they have tended to ask for very high interest rates and arrangement fees.

It seems that, in a similar way to large investment institutions, smaller quoted businesses are often considered too fiddly in a world where there are many larger borrowers ready to do a deal. Hence, banks have been content to lose their market share in this part of the market. The differential in the large and smaller companies' access to credit has got even worse since-2008. Many banks have tended to shrink their balance sheets to boost the percentage of capital reserves and meet the increased requirements post 2008. This trend has had an adverse effect on many smaller companies in the UK, including many in the quoted smaller company sector. A large number of smaller quoted businesses have no debt at all, which contrasts greatly with the position for almost all the larger companies.

Given that the rate of corporate expansion is related, in part, to the ease with which businesses have access to finance, it might be expected that large companies have enjoyed a period of above-average returns in the last twenty-five years compared with smaller companies. Since the credit boom started in 1985, the trend of smaller company outperformance has been obscured. (See Appendix 6, page 149 for full rationale.) Many of those businesses that had good access to the new forms of debt have performed extremely well and the largest companies generally have delivered attractive returns. But, as might be expected, the companies that were medium-sized, but still had access to the new forms of debt performed better. Much better. Medium-sized companies outperformed the largest companies because they had the double advantage of good access to debt that boosted their performance as well as benefiting from an element of the smaller company effect.

The fact that the small company effect – where small would be expected to outperform – has been partially obscured by the credit boom is an important conclusion for the Slow Investor. Remember that the favoured Slow criteria include opting to invest in smaller companies, with a general inclination to apply the mantra 'the smaller the better'. As the effect of the credit boom has held up the natural outperformance of smaller companies, smaller companies might be expected to outperform in the coming years as the smaller company effect reasserts itself. In addition, companies that are relatively under-borrowed are also likely to see a catch-up in their performance. Many quoted smaller companies fit both of these criteria.

Now – this is important – the size premium is already reasserting itself.[8] Not just in the UK, but in nineteen countries around the world, representing the bulk of total global stock market capitalisation. The opening years of the twenty-first century were seen as a 'lost decade' for equity markets, but this was mainly due to markets peaking around the year 2000 and the poor

---

8   Dimson, E, Marsh, P Stauton, M (2011) *Credit Suisse Global Investment Returns Sourcebook* p. 44 London Business School

performance of some of the world's largest companies in the credit crunch.[9] Small has been beautiful. Small is still beautiful. Perhaps we have missed that point in the fever of excitement and chaotic moments of recent years.

Timing and small: institutional interest in the smaller company universe

When the RBS HGSC Index[10] was launched in 1987, the premium returns on offer from smaller companies were historically large. Institutions naturally assumed that the previous trend would go forward uninterrupted. During 1987 and 1988, many institutions bought into the small-cap story, and the allocation of this capital to a relatively illiquid part of the market led to a further period of outperformance by the smaller company universe. At that time, the excitement about the small-company sector led to the issue of many dedicated smaller company funds. In addition, many pension funds allocated a dedicated portion of their UK equity exposure to smaller companies.

With the benefit of hindsight, it's now possible to recognise that the early stages of the credit boom were just lapping at the markets at that time. This trend was ultimately to benefit mid- and larger-sized companies and relatively disadvantage smaller companies. Moreover, with the UK in the European Exchange Rate Mechanism (ERM), interest rates in the late 1980s and early 1990s had to be progressively raised in an attempt to keep the sterling exchange rate in line with that required for the ERM. The UK entered recession and this also adversely affected the performance of the smaller and micro-cap companies. These companies had a disproportionate percentage of their operations in the local economy compared to the average larger international company.

Both these factors were disadvantageous to the average smaller company. As a result, the FTSE Small Cap index tended to underperform during this period. Following the suspension of sterling's membership of the ERM in September 1992, the UK economy did receive a boost to growth compared to other economies as our exchange and interest rates fell back. The FTSE Small Cap enjoyed a good year in 1993, but thereafter the credit boom handed the advantage to larger companies for an extended period. The

---

9   MSCI World Small-cap index outperformed the MSCI World large-cap index by a significant margin

10 RBS Hoare Govett Smaller Companies Index

failure of the AIM market to outperform following its issue in 1996, and the continued underperformance of the FTSE Small Cap in the decade from 2000 to 2010, disappointed those investors who had expected outperformance from stocks at the bottom end of the market. Institutional interest in the sector faded. And after the dotcom boom in 1999, the best performance over the last ten years has been in the FTSE 250.

So institutional interest has fallen away from the underperforming smaller company sector, and new capital was allocated into those areas that were performing well, particularly those in the FTSE 250 index. The outperformance of mid-sized stocks is highly advantageous for large financial institutions. The Mid Cap index only comprises 250 stocks, so this universe of stocks is very much easier for professionals to monitor than the 1500 or so small and micro-cap companies. And, given that some are large enough to be on the doorstep of the FTSE 100, there's a lot of daily trading in their shares. This makes it easy for institutional portfolios to be adjusted at will should they need to invest or disinvest capital. Institutional interest has grown and grown in the FTSE 250.

Meanwhile, earlier expectations of ongoing outperformance by the smaller and micro-cap companies universe have been replaced by some institutional frustration when withdrawing cash from these tiny stocks. To many institutional fund managers, 'smaller companies' is an anathema. They've been there, have the scars to prove it and they have taken every opportunity to cash in smaller-company investments of the past. This is clearly evident in the flows of investment in and out of the unitised investment vehicles.[11] In a period when capital allocation to unitised vehicles has been strong, both institutional and retail investors have been progressively withdrawing capital year after year.

Institutional interest in the small and micro-cap sector is exceptionally low. This is reflected in the valuations of smaller companies' investment trusts, many of which stand at a sizable discount to their underlying assets. If, however, the world is going ex-growth and returns from larger companies are closely linked to the rate of world economic growth, then financial institutions have the makings of a big problem. Returns from giant portfolios of larger companies could be unexceptional at best. While some mid-sized companies may find some areas where they can continue to expand in a world that is not growing, these will be few in number. As it is,

---

11 Pooled investment structure

most institutional portfolios are already overweight in these businesses and so it is unlikely that they will be able to allocate a lot more institutional capital to these. Many institutions may find themselves compelled, almost by default, to reconsider those areas where they are least weighted – the small and micro-cap sectors.

The ceasing of the institutional withdrawals from the sector is already a significant change. That alone might be sufficient to re-establish the normal pattern of small and micro-cap stocks outperforming by a sizable degree. The patterns of the past would restart at almost the same moment that the credit boom comes to an end. Watching the discount on smaller companies' investment trusts would be a good way to monitor developments. As soon as there is a suggestion that there is money to be made in these trusts, prices may move to premium versus their underlying asset values – which, in itself, could prove a disincentive for other prospective buyers!

Over the period of the credit boom, institutions have progressively moved away from the most illiquid stocks in the stock market. Clearly, portfolio liquidity is an important factor when determining the make-up of an institutional portfolio. But investments that are small and fiddly cannot be ignored in a world where economic growth may be constrained, and where attractive investment returns may be difficult to come by. Institutions tend to move slowly and it may take some time for them to recognise that they will need to take a degree of liquidity risk in at least a part of their portfolio. Liquidity as a factor shouldn't automatically preclude investing in a full range of investments. The Slow Investor, having constructed a portfolio based on the favourable factors that include stocks with smaller market capitalisations ahead of the institutions' change of heart, would be the greatest beneficiary of this change.

The appeal of value

Over the longer term, returns from value investing have outstripped those from following growth strategies by a significant margin. There is broad agreement that concentrating investments on businesses that are modestly priced because they face challenging situations – in mature markets or facing setbacks – can reap rewards.[12] There is less agreement over whether premium

---

12 See Fama E, French, F (1998) *Value versus growth: The International Evidence 1975-1999* Journal of Finance 53 (6)

performance simply reflects that these investments carry a higher degree of risk. In spite of its long-term success, as a strategy it has also suffered some quite extensive setbacks. The 1990s, for example, were a particularly strong period for growth stocks. This was the period in which globalisation really accelerated, when the overall cost of finance was declining, and it made sense for companies to borrow to grow. Access to finance for companies that were perceived to be front runners really accelerated, and enthusiasm for the growth stories seemed undimmed. Once again, understanding the economic environment and access to credit is vital.

The appeal of the value strategy today lies in the way it acknowledges stock market volatility and encourages investors to try to profit from it. Growth is more vulnerable to heightened expectations that can be dashed. At a time when there is greater uncertainty about economic outcomes as QE comes to an end, the relevance of strategy that seeks a margin of safety is obvious. However after the market recovery to mid-2011, there are relatively few stocks that are intrinsically cheap, as QE has been effective in reinvigorating financial markets again after the credit crisis. In fact, strict followers of Graham's investment regime would be recommending increasing allocations to defensive assets like gilts, and awaiting a correction. Remember that he suggested that the proportion of equities could vary between 25 per cent and 75 per cent of the portfolio, depending on market conditions.

While the value strategy can have impact on its own, real synergy lies in combination with small-cap. Here the evidence from the historic record in the UK seems quite overwhelming. It would be expected that UK companies that combine both the small and value criteria would outperform large growth stocks in the wider, listed universe, but the amount of outperformance indicated by research from the London Business School is quite remarkable. Analysis of returns shows that small value outstripped all the other classifications (big value, small growth, big growth) between 1955 and 2010. Returns from small value produce returns almost **one hundred fold greater** than big growth in this study.[13]

- £1 invested in 1956 would become £20,855 by 2010 with a small value strategy.
- £1 invested in big growth at the same time would become £245.

---

13 See Dimson, E, Marsh, P, Stanton, M (2011) *Credit Suisse Global Investment Returns Sourcebook* p. 49 for methodology for study for the period 1955-2010

As with all these calculations, the cost of transactions has not been included, but they underline just how attractive it is for the Slow Investor to combine the strategies outlined in this book.

The power of good and growing dividends

Fifty years ago it was suggested that investors should not be too concerned about dividends – whether their income was paid out in the form of dividends or received as a capital gain.[14] The idea was that if investors received too little in dividends, but their stock appreciated, they could sell some shares to make up the difference. In fact, dividends do seem to matter, worth 'more in the hand' than capital retained on the balance sheet. And it is a central principle of Slow finance that they will become more important for investors in the coming years.

During the credit boom, it was striking that many of the fastest growing companies paid no dividends, and some larger businesses reduced their dividend payout ratios too.[15] There was a perception that investing to grow could be an effective way of delivering shareholder value, and that a generous payout somehow signaled a lack of management drive or innovative ideas. Now, in a slower growth world, payout strategies could change. *Slow Finance* anticipates that more investors will seek premium returns without relying upon multiple transactions. And history shows that returns from high-yielding portfolios have outstripped low yielders by a solid margin, both overseas[16] and in the UK.[17]

- £1 invested in a high yield strategy in 1900 would have become £100,160 by 2010.
- The same amount in low yielders would return £5122.

How domestic investing fell out of favour

As growth has accelerated in emerging and frontier economies after 1985, the proportion of capital that institutions have invested outside the UK has accelerated. In 1985, UK assets made up around two-thirds of all

---

14 Miller, H.M, Modigliani, F (1961) *Dividend Policy, Growth and The Valuation of Shares* Journal of Business, (34) pp. 411-433

15 The Economist *Dividends' end* 10.01.2002

16 Dimson, E, Marsh, P, Stanton, M (2011) *Credit Suisse Global Investment Returns Sourcebook* London Business School p. 18 1975-2010; data supplied by French, K

17 Dimson, E, Marsh, P, Stanton, M (2011) *Credit Suisse Global Investment Returns Sourcebook* p. 18 London Business School p. 18 UK 1900-2010

pension assets. Just over twenty years later, it had dropped to less than 40 per cent.[18] Domestic investing is out of favour, in spite of the fact that recent competition from overseas and a weaker currency have helped make the UK more competitive again. While there are clearly benefits from diversification, it's important to recognise that seeking to invest in high growth economies may not bring premium returns.

It *is* true that the UK is unlikely to see its economic fortune improve dramatically in the near term, but it does not mean that investment opportunities will be impossible to find. As a class that is broadly out of favour, perhaps the opposite applies. The principles of Slow finance highlight the idea that the strategy of investing locally can be a win-win situation. Financing local companies can help generate local employment, and foster the kind of co-operative values that are clearly valued in the wider community but have been increasingly overlooked in the last twenty-five years in finance.

There is also growing literature that explores whether using local knowledge – of one's own or of a locally based professional – makes financial sense too. Here, the evidence is much less dramatic in scale than that suggested by the other strategies, but even small amounts of outperformance should not be disregarded. Research from Harvard suggests that individuals who are geographically close to the assets in which they invest may have an information edge, which can translate into a modest degree of outperformance.[19] This work concentrates on equity research and the proximity to information sources, and the impact of intermediaries like underwriters in the information chain. Being proximate can help.

Of course, this broad concept can be used in action outside complex information chains. A good example of this is demonstrated by the London property investment company Shaftesbury plc. The managers have a policy of only investing within walking distance of the company's office in central London. They can walk their estate every day to address issues as soon as they become apparent. For me, it is not unrelated to the fact that Shaftesbury has been one of the very best performing property companies over the last twenty-five years.[20] To some extent, this seems common-sense. Having an in-depth knowledge of what you are investing in and of being able to see what is happening on the ground must surely help to develop a

---

18 WM All Funds Universe, State Street Investment Analytics Asset Allocation 1985-2009

19 Malloy, C (2003) *The Geography of Equity Analysis* Harvard Business School, NBER

20 My belief in this strategy means that I have invested on my own behalf in this company. As at June 2011

view that is more insightful than someone located on the other side of the globe. Feedforward signals – which may be as simple as how busy someone's premises look – don't have to be complicated. These are features that Slow Investors should seek to exploit.

Fig 8.1: Following a Slow investment strategy

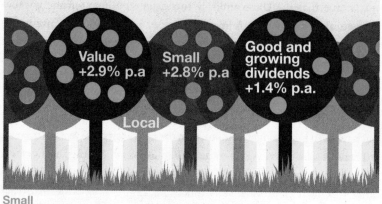

Small
UK RBS HGSC, premium vs. FTSE All-Share 1955-2010
Value
US High book-to-market, premium vs. Market Average 1926-2010
Good and growing dividends
UK High yield, premium vs. FTSE All-Share 1900-2010

Source: Elroy Dimson, Paul Marsh and Mike Staunton, *CS Global Investment Returns Sourcebook 2011*
Copyright © 2011 Gervais Williams

With strategies in context, it's now time to get to work and think of how to frame investment decisions. When making any decisions of this kind, it's always important to consider when you actually commit capital to your investment selection. That's an important moment. In 2008, for example, any stock market investment made at the start of the year would probably have fallen in value quite sharply by December. Investors were shocked and surprised by many events during that year and many were forced to liquidate their holdings, as many had used borrowed money to purchase investments. As share prices fell, they were obliged to sell the holdings, even if they believed they were too cheap, in order to use the proceeds to repay the debt. In contrast, if you had purchased your investment during the last quarter of that year, then it's very likely that the share price of your investment would have risen during 2009 as the stock market recovered. Most investors would not have had the confidence to buy during that period, as many commentators were highlighting the risk that many of the UK high street banks might face insolvency. The timing of your investment can, quite clearly, affect the return on it.

As the Bank of England scales back the implementation of QE and possibly increases interest rates, it's quite plausible that stock markets may gyrate in the following years. In early 2011, the UK stock market had staged a very substantial recovery from the lows in October 2008, reaching close to a new absolute high. One of Benjamin Graham's three principles recommends that investors profit from market volatility to enhance their investment return. Given that markets have risen so sharply from recent lows, Slow Investors should be cautious about committing too large a part of their savings to such a market. Should the stock market fall back in due course, at that stage it would be more advantageous to consider allocating a larger percentage of savings to the Slow Investor strategy.

The problem in deciding when to transact is that decisions are based upon factors that are simply unknowable. Is the stock market close to a turning point, or could it continue to fall back for a longer period? Investors fret over this issue. The big advantage of a strategy that focuses upon stock selection, such as that advocated in this book, is that the investor's attention is mainly focused upon factors that are to some degree knowable. Identifying those businesses that fall into the value definition, that have the prospect of good and growing dividends, a small market capitalisation and are relatively local to the investor are factors that over time may be expected to lead to a premium investment return. And it's anticipated that these trends will hold good for the future. Yes, the timing of the investment transaction will have a significant effect on the short-term performance. However, with the progress of time, the accrued return on the investment becomes proportionally the more important component of return. Therefore, to some degree, irrespective of whether the investments were purchased somewhat ahead of, or just after, a market bottom, the accrued return to the investor on the Slow Investor strategy should be highly attractive.

Timing: can momentum guide a Slow sell strategy?

When to sell is a key issue for any investor, including a Slow one. With this in mind, there's one more strategy that may be of interest, and that's momentum.[21] This might seem strange in a book that advocates a value bias in stock selection, as value is all about buying stocks at times when they are close to new lows. Momentum, on the other hand, is all about 'making the trend your friend', buying stocks when they are already running up and therefore moving towards what could be new highs. It has to be recognised that trends in share prices do develop. Individual stocks can outperform (or underperform) relative to the remainder of the stock market for a long period.

The momentum of a share price can be measured using a wide range of different rules to assess the stocks that have momentum against those that don't. The most common momentum strategy suggests that investors look to buy companies that have outperformed in the previous twelve months, having waited for one month to check that this is still valid before transacting.[22] The new investment can then be checked monthly to see whether it still falls in the 'buy stocks' category a month later. Momentum works well in stock markets that are trending in one direction for some years. But, at times of stock market turns, the strategy tends to buy into stocks that have had momentum in the past and, given the market turn, these tend to be the ones that subsequently underperform. Momentum strategies therefore take up to twelve months to catch up with the new trends in the market. Another drawback with a momentum strategy is that stocks with buy signals have to outperform in the period *prior* to being identified as potentially attractive investments. And, as with all share prices, sometimes a company will outperform for reasons that might persist for many years, or they might outperform because of a short-term speculative reason that doesn't persist at all. So with a momentum strategy, it's quite possible for investors who buy stocks to be given a sell signal shortly afterwards and take a loss.

Even so, the differential in performance for the most common set of momentum rules is highly impressive. The LBS professors have calculated that using this strategy added 7.7 per cent a year in the 110-year period between 1900 and 2010.[23] The strategy identifies stocks that have

---

21 Momentum: An investment strategy that aims to take advantage of established trends e.g. buying established stock market 'winners' over a specified time period

22 This method has been backtested against stock market data, and is the most widely adopted by academics

23 Dimson, E, Marsh, P, Stanton, M (2011) *Credit Suisse Global Investment Returns Sourcebook* p. 49 London Business School

outperformed in the past, so it does offer the investor a better chance than normal to get involved in a stock that is about to outperform for a sustained period. But there's also a reasonable chance that the investor could be buying a stock that has bounced up well above its intrinsic value and is about to fall back too.

For me, one of the main downsides of momentum strategies is that they normally involve a large number of individual transactions to make them work. Transactions can be expensive and time-consuming, more so for the individual than the institutional investor. Buying and selling shares in individual companies many times over, without necessarily producing a good return because of the significant dealing costs, is not attractive for a Slow Investor on so many levels. I believe the risk/reward ratio of the momentum strategy is not as intrinsically well founded as the others described in this book. It also tends to deliver sizable losses at turning points in the market.

However, stocks advocated by this book's strategy may well be the unwitting beneficiaries of the momentum effect. Favoured stocks are highlighted, hopefully, as they come towards the end of a period of underperformance and therefore ahead of a period of outperformance. Many of the investment purchases may have been made prior to the stock having upward share price momentum. But if they are successful investments, then they might well subsequently start to fall into the category of stocks that deliver the best performance in the momentum strategy too. Therefore, the momentum strategy may offer the Slow Investor a check for a 'sell' discipline, rather than a 'buy' discipline. This helps address a key issue for the Slow Investor. In the case of the steel construction company Severfield Rowen, the ideal holding period was over fifteen years! Given the very sizable profits available for the investor during that period, it would have been easy to take significant profits frequently, thereby exiting the holding at a much too early stage.

So the 'sell' signals of the momentum strategy may be a useful check to the Slow Investor whereas the 'buy' signals can be ignored. This means the Slow Investor can keep their holdings for a longer period than otherwise might be the case. In time, the Slow Investor will tend to find new investments that are more attractive than those already held, and therefore the holding period will be self limiting in this regard. By combining the strategies, the Slow Investor can use the momentum 'sell' signal as a reminder that their investment has probably moved out of the value category and is overdue to sell. It could be that using the 'best of both' offers the Slow Investor the highest premium returns.

If the Slow Investor is looking to monitor the 'sell' discipline, then a current holding should be sold when it falls into the worst 30 per cent of underperformers over a twelve-month period.[24] For the Slow Investor, this indicator can be used to indicate that an investment may have already matured, if it hasn't been sold previously.

Combining investment strategies for Active Slow Investors

Now that the Active Slow Investor has an established approach to use to narrow the pool of potential stocks in which to invest, and some guidance on when to buy and sell, the next challenge is where to source information. This can be problematic for non-professional investors. To address the problem, an App has been developed to help Active Slow Investors to identify the optimum group of investments.

The App contains a database of all the quoted companies in the UK and gives the location of all the major operations of quoted companies. It identifies the fifty closest businesses to the user, using the investor's own location. For those investors in a relatively lowly populated part of the country, these companies might be within a twenty-five-mile range. For those in a major urban environment, the fifty companies might all lie within a range of less than five miles.

The Active Slow Investor isn't solely interested in the nearest businesses, but rather in identifying local businesses that meet some of the favourable investment strategies. The App lists the fifty local businesses together with an indication of how well they also incorporate the three remaining favoured factors. The investor can choose which of those factors are most relevant to them. For investors who are particularly keen on dividend yield, the App will highlight the ten best dividend payers in the list of the fifty nearest companies. For those who are interested in selecting on the basis of the value criteria, then the ten best will be highlighted, as will the market capitalisation information for those wishing to select on the smallness criteria.

From the information displayed, it will be obvious which companies are amongst the best on other criteria and also evident to the user if a business

---

24 Dimson, E, Marsh, P, Stanton, M (2011) *Credit Suisse Global Investment Returns Sourcebook* p. 49 London Business School

were to meet three of the favoured criteria. It's worth highlighting that the selection criteria are all based on the sample of fifty companies initially selected on the locality of the investor. The merits of each criterion are not calculated on an absolute basis, but are relative to the group of the fifty companies nearest to the investor. On occasions, there will be companies that meet the criteria of more than one of these attractive strategies simultaneously. Meeting one or more of the criteria doesn't automatically guarantee that such a business will outperform, but it does imply that the chances of it outperforming are greater than other stocks that meet none or only one of those criteria.

Notes of caution: risk and diversification

It's vital to note that the ultimate decision on whether to invest is not made solely on the information contained within the App. It is a tool to help the Slow Investor focus their search for quoted businesses that might meet the favoured criteria, but **it is the responsibility of the investor to carry out further research.** If you're an inexperienced investor, it's advisable to seek help from others.

Before the Active Slow Investor makes an investment decision, I recommend gaining a good understanding of the balance sheet of the business, including its debt profile. As the credit boom comes to an end, a long period of credit constraint is likely to persist, which could mean that companies with higher debt levels find they are unable to maintain their bank facilities. At best, such companies are likely to have to compromise on their investment plans and, at worst, such businesses might be in danger of going into receivership and become worthless for shareholders. The App does not include a company's debt profile as the data is not always as transparent as might be assumed. Even smaller quoted companies use a range of different methods to borrow, from bank overdrafts to invoice discounting and leasing agreements.[25] Slow Investors are advised to ensure they have a full understanding of the risks associated with accumulated debt when making investment decisions. As highlighted earlier, there are many quoted companies that have no net borrowing and even those with modest net borrowings may represent good investments.

---

25 Leasing agreements, which allow use of equipment or premises in exchange for regular cash payments, may last for some years.

Finally, the Slow Investor, like all other investors, needs to be sure to spread their investment capital. Benjamin Graham suggested that all investors should hold some capital in government bonds, so that the investor can profit from the volatility of the stock market. In addition to this, it's advisable for the Slow Investor to invest in a series of different companies. 'Don't put all your eggs in one basket' is the well-known phrase that comes to mind. Early research suggested that, as a very minimum, fifteen largely equally-weighted holdings are required to diversify stock-specific risk. This assumes that the different investments are all in very different industries and that the problems of one aren't likely to be duplicated in others. For practical purposes, twenty-five largely equally-weighted holdings is a better number. This has the advantage of spreading stock-specific risk while still leaving plenty of scope for significant performance if the individual stocks are well selected.

Using Slow as a guide

This chapter addresses what those outside the financial sector can do to mitigate the risks on their own savings, and engage with a practical strategy with potential to offer premium returns. For Active Slow Investors, there are established themes that can be explored, back-tested against many years of stock market data, which help to reduce the field of potential investments. These are stocks that are more attractive in terms of value, dividend income, smallness and those that are local in terms of orientation. It's hoped that by selecting from this pool that the Active Slow Investor will have the best chance of receiving premium returns in what might be a challenging economic period. As data on these features is not always available easily for non-financial investors, there is an App to help investors to identify those companies that meet predetermined criteria.

The Slow approach is not solely about taking decisions as an individual. It's about how individuals come together as a community. Having savings is a privilege, but with such privilege comes responsibility. The Slow Investor recognises that this involves taking a closer interest in how our assets are allocated. Maximising potential return is only half the story. The Slow Investor also understands that one privilege of holding an investment in an individual stock is also about exercising a small degree of influence, and acting as an owner. The legendary investor Benjamin Graham knew this, and his wisdom is just as valid now as it was all those years ago.

CONCLUSIONS: THE COMING OF SLOW FINANCE

Our progression through recent economic history has provided an insight into how economies have developed since the mid-eighties. Borrowing has increased substantially beyond long-term norms. At the international scale, the global economy appears to be running at two speeds. The activities of the real economy are bridged to a supersized financial sector by almost one quadrillion dollars of inter-bank transactions. Over the last twenty-five years financial models have optimised and re-optimised the utilisation of capital, facilitating almost infinitely liquid exchanges. The financial sector has its own momentum, its own agenda, and as it becomes more intricate, generates apparently superb profits.

But as it has become global, it has lost connection with the societies it was created to serve. It has reached a level of sophistication where savers are intermediated from their savings by layers of financial professionals. Individual investors are disempowered. Their views and those from outside the financial sector carry little weight in the way in which capital is allocated. Investors often do not wish to pursue high-risk strategies based upon quick-fire transactions, to use cheap debt to magnify returns or follow growth strategies that are not transparent or easy to understand.

Together, these trends have brought the global financial system to the point of crisis. The credit boom that has generated much of this activity is unsustainable. The financial crisis of 2008 was a wake-up call, but that call has been largely disregarded. A false sense of security is being given by artificial measures that are keeping the cost of borrowing low and money circulating in the economy. Lord Turner of the Financial Services Authority is asking whether we are being radical enough in the reforming of financial services,[1] and has observed that not enough time is being spent assessing the social value of financial activity.

---

1   Turner, A (2011) *Reforming Finance: Are we being radical enough?* Clare Distinguished Lecture in Economics and Public Policy, Cambridge University, 18.02.11

While this debate is played out at high level among the policy makers, I see a significant change in orientation *driven by individual savers*; a major attitude shift in core values and beliefs in the coming years. This is likely to involve individuals seeking a more direct say in the allocation of their investments; taking greater responsibility for their own financial health and more interest in how assets are managed on their behalf. In short, a renewed interest in the connection between the investor and the investment.

It is the excesses of previous financial trends that will inform the new values. The previous excessive complexity of novel financial products will drive a renewed desire for investment simplicity. The overuse of debt will be replaced with a desire to avoid the instability associated with excessive credit. A move away from hoping to get lucky on trading gains in the next high growth economy or commodity will be replaced with a renewed interest in good and growing dividend income. Fast strategies based upon uncertain market liquidity will be replaced by a renewed emphasis on compounding returns over time. After decades where bigger seemed better, investors will readopt an interest in smallness and stock specific selection.

The appeal of these principles lies in the fact that they reconnect the investor and the ultimate purpose of investing. They hand more control back to the investor. They offer scope to re-invigorate companies that have suffered reduced access to capital during the credit boom. They can help boost the domestic economy and local employment. But the Slow investment strategy still offers the prospect of premium returns. Investing in Value, in smaller domestic companies, in high dividend not high growth markets and in companies with good and growing income are all strategies that have delivered over the long term.

These changes in orientation seem inevitable; finance has become excessively complex, global and high-powered. But as an industry it seems curiously ill-prepared for the end of the credit boom and the knock-on effects in products which have been over-engineered for capital efficiency rather than margin for error.

The *Slow Finance* perspective offers a catalyst to anticipate these changes, and an alternative paradigm for sustainable investing. The *Slow Finance* principles[2] form a road map for investors to go forward where straightforward investment logic happily coexists with the wider interests of others.

---

2   See Chapter 2

Postscript

Within *Slow Finance* there is a strong sense that the investment world is on the cusp of a major period of change. Anticipating the timing of that change or the specific sequence of events was problematic even as recently as June 2011. However, whilst the book was prepared for publication, a series of key announcements have followed in quick succession.

Firstly, it has been formally acknowledged that Greece will default on its debt – the first sovereign default of a Western European nation for more than fifty years. Members of the Eurozone are grappling with the tensions within the single currency area and fears about the health of the European banking sector have reemerged. And, while the US Government narrowly avoided default on its borrowings, it has been divided by disagreement over how to reduce its dependence on debt-funded expansion within an economy that is already heavily-indebted. These events have contributed to all kinds of new, sometimes uncomfortable, 'firsts'. The first time America has lost it AAA rating, and the implication that there might be further downgrades in future; the first period in which the FTSE-100 lost more than 100 points in four sessions in a row; the first time the price of gold jumped over 1,850 dollars an ounce; and the introduction of government austerity in an environment of falling real wages, which has catalyzed a new range of social challenges in the UK.

In my view, these events are significant. Though the largest credit boom in history was ultimately unsustainable at least the issue is now becoming more widely recognised and discussed. We now know the future years will differ from those of the last twenty five, as we all begin the long process of unwinding. Whilst this is a scenario full of uncertainty, there is greater scope for us as citizens and savers to influence how the financial world should assist in the process. Perversely, it is the very uncertainty that offers all of us a more meaningful hand in what the future might look like. This period of change applies equally to the headlong trends of allocating capital to the attractions of globalisation and chasing rapid growth.

These issues are important since the decisions we make can be expected to have a profound effect on the shape of our economy. The previous focus was on the relatively narrow theme of massive scale and steroid-type growth took unacceptable risks with our national balance sheet. Transacting more and more frequently, particularly with increasingly large sums in distant territories, is now progressively being seen as something of an investment cul-de-sac. So how should we best allocate our savings beyond the credit boom? What factors should have significant weight in this process? Slow Finance explores these questions in the context of the wider responsibilities of investment; a viable approach that can deliver enhanced domestic economic growth and local employment through the allocation of our savings. It highlights the importance of localism through the introduction of the concept of Investment Miles, as well as advocating the previously overlooked advantages of the compounding of dividends, the reuse of older assets through value strategies, and the potential within smallness. The deeply unsettled financial trends that are coming through as this book goes to print only underline the relevance of these strategies. I anticipate there will be a lot more discussion from a range of perspectives regarding our investment options for the future, as we seek the best path forward. It is hoped that *Slow Finance* will make a constructive contribution to this vital debate.

Gervais Williams, 19th August 2011

Appendices

1: WHAT IS A CDO?

2: HOW DOES QUANTITATIVE EASING WORK?

3: THE EVOLUTION OF THE OTC SWAP MARKET

4: EVALUATING VALUE INVESTING

5: POUND-COST AVERAGING

6: SMALLER COMPANIES, ACCESS TO DEBT AND IMPLICATIONS FOR HISTORIC STOCK MARKET PERFORMANCE

APPENDIX 1

What is a CDO?

A Collateralised Debt Obligation (CDO) is a pooled investment fund, based on underlying debt assets which could include mortgages, credit card debt, car loans etc. These are packaged and sold in parts or tranches to investors.

Aim: To match loans so that the risks of default in one type of loan would be uncorrelated with the others in a tiered structure.

Intention: To manage and offer appropriate levels of risk. CDOs offer investors a 'menu' of different risk profiles, according to investors' 'appetite' for risk.

Structure: The tiered structure meant that it was anticipated that losses from any loans that defaulted could be contained more effectively. Low risk investors could buy into debt structured from the lowest-risk tier, so it was believed they could be sheltered from the negative implications of defaults in higher-risk tiers.

Interest payments structured according to risk.

APPENDIX 2

How does Quantitative Easing work?

QE involves the electronic creation of money. It works in two ways:

Improving the flow of money via asset purchases

The central bank buys assets, like government bonds, from private sector organisations, e.g. banks, pension funds, insurance companies.

To do so, it uses 'new' money created by itself, the central bank.

This gives institutions capital that earns little as interest rates are low. Many choose to reallocate this capital to other parts of the economy, funding economic activities that have come to a halt.

Examples:
Funding rights issues of quoted businesses trying to repay excessive debt;
Funding investment plans;
Enabling banks to rebuild their capital safety margin and re-start lending.

Indirectly reducing borrowing costs

The government itself competes to buy government bonds. The price of the bonds goes up, so the yield on the bonds consequently falls (See Chapter 5, page 77).

QE keeps bond yields low, reducing the government's own borrowing costs.

In doing so, it makes other bond investments less attractive than they would otherwise be.

In turn, other types of investments, like shares and commodities, become relatively more attractive.

APPENDIX 3

The evolution of the OTC swap market

OTC transactions are arranged directly between banks, and are often simple in concept.

Financial swaps were initiated after World War II, when international capital controls were in place. Capital controls could prevent a bank translating a payment it had received back into its home currency. This represented a risk, as the bank had no control over how two currencies could diverge in the future.

On occasions, banks found that they had matching problems. One may have received a payment in UK sterling and its home currency was US dollars. The second may have had the reverse position. Neither was permitted to resolve the situation by a foreign exchange transaction.

The financial innovation was to agree a contract to swap the movement of the currency differences in the future. At set dates, perhaps every month or every quarter, the difference in valuation between the two currencies could be settled by a cash payment between them.

If the foreign currency held rose in value over the three months, then the notional 'profit' would be paid to the other bank or counterparty. This would offset the equal notional 'loss' made by the counterparty.

The original underlying currency position stayed with the original banks. Only the *difference* in the currency valuations was paid in cash – swapped – between them.

In the mid-1980s, financial trading volumes increased and dealers became more willing to make tighter bid/offer spreads (i.e. the difference between a bid to buy and the offer to sell became smaller). It also became possible to trade larger and larger lot sizes. Currency controls of the past were removed, but the increased volumes of trading in the markets stimulated a new use for swaps.

Finance directors of large international companies could source the cheapest loans on international markets, and then 'swap' the currency risk back to the desired currency as the deal completed. In this way, larger businesses enjoyed lower cost loans, and the currency risk was removed through the 'swap' market.

Over the last twenty-five years, this type of transaction has become more and more popular, and led to great sophistication in the OTC swap market. There are now established markets for swapping interest payments to and from variable rates of interest.

Most recently, a swap market has developed based on the risk of default of the underlying lender. These swaps are known as Credit Default Swaps (CDSs). Now there are opportunities for the lender of a corporate loan, or indeed the borrower, to swap out the currency risk, the interest rate risk and the default risk. For the lender, this represents an apparently near riskless series of interest payments on the principal until the loan matures.

APPENDIX 4

Evaluating Value Investing

Question: Do Value stocks really outperform Growth stocks?

Question: How can relative performance be measured?

Economists Eugene Fama and Kenneth French, later joined by James Davies, are best known for their work measuring if Value investing could deliver enhanced returns.[1,2] (i.e. backing 'also-ran' companies, not those perceived to be fast growing leaders).

To do this, they needed to find a way of consistently defining **value stocks**, relative to all other stocks, whatever the level of the overall equity market.

They decided to use the notion of **book value**[3] to define value. This is closely connected with the concept of **intrinsic value**[4] first outlined by Graham.

The ratio of the book value of a business was divided by the market capitalisation to determine those stocks that had the highest relative value.

Businesses with a lot of assets, combined with relatively low market capitalisation, would be the closest to the intrinsically cheap stocks that Graham had advocated. In contrast, those companies with very few assets on their balance sheet versus their market capitalisation would most closely match those that Graham advocated should be sold.

For clarity, such businesses were defined as **Growth** stocks. These are fashionable investments, where optimism over their potential future performance has driven up their share prices against their book values.

---

1   Fama, E.F, French, K.R (1992) *The Cross-Section of Expected Stock Returns* Journal of Finance XLVII (2) June 1992

2   Davies, J.L, Fama, E.F, French, K.R (2000) *Characteristics, Covariances and Average Returns 1929–1997* Journal of Finance LV (1)

3   Value of an asset on the balance sheet, after depreciation and amortisation of relevant costs

4   Intrinsic value, for Graham, involved using the formula: *Value = Current (Normal) Earnings x (8.5 + (2 x Expected Annual Growth Rate over next 7–10 years)*

The term 'growth stocks' was a fairly loose term in this context. Fama and French did not include any information on the sales trends of the business, or the rate of growth of these sales in classification. They are perceived to be most in demand, since they just might be big companies of the future. 'Growth' is a relatively accurate description in this context.

By listing all of the businesses in order of the book to market capitalisation ratio, those at the top would be those with the highest relative Value. They would be relatively 'cheap'.

Those at the bottom would be those with least relative Value. They would be relatively 'expensive', but therefore perhaps the most fashionable at the time.

The list was divided into three groups, with approximately equal sums of total market capitalisation in each. The data was calculated using data from previous years. At the end of the period, the overall performance of each group of stocks could be measured.

The difference between the Value stocks (the group at the top of list) versus Growth stocks (the group at the bottom of the list) delivers a single figure of the relative performance of these groups each year. The performance of the middle group was discarded. If there were a consistently positive differential then Graham's thesis would be valid.

The longest running time series study[5] examined prices on the New York Stock Exchange between 1929 and 1997, recalculating the relative value of each stock every year, and then measuring the differential in performance of the relative Value group against the relative Growth group.

On average, Value stocks outperformed Growth stocks by between 0.4 and 0.5 per cent *each month*.

---

5   Davies, J.L, Fama, E.F, French, K.R (2000) *Characteristics, Covariances and Average Returns 1929–1997* Journal of Finance LV (1)

APPENDIX 5

Pound-cost averaging

An ideal strategy for an investor seeking to make a gradual change in asset allocation.

How does it work?

It works through buying assets at predetermined regular intervals with equal amounts of capital.

Benefit

The investor does not have to worry that they are buying at any particular period when the asset price is at a small peak, since they are only buying a small percentage each time. It leads to a **weighted-average purchase price**. Pound-cost averaging softens the responsibility for getting the investment timing exactly right. It can be particularly helpful when the price of the asset being bought may be moving to slip lower. Precision investors often set a predetermined price to buy an asset and may miss out on investing if the predetermined price is never actually reached in the market. The pound-cost average investor *al ways* gets their investment at a time of their choosing.

APPENDIX 6

Smaller companies, access to debt and implications for historic stock market performance

In the last twenty-five years, access to finance (including debt finance) appears to have played a role in explaining relative stock market performance.

Slow Investors may be interested in identifying what has differentiated small companies with good access to debt and those who have been relatively debt-constrained. This can be achieved through analysis of different stock market indices representing different groups of small companies, whose performance has varied in recent history.

The highest profile market is that of the Alternative Investment Market or AIM, which came into existence in 1996. AIM has been highly successful in attracting new listings of small and micro-cap companies, but the overall return of this market since it started has been zero. Returns on AIM have been undermined by a lot of fashionable stocks being issued at high valuations during the dotcom boom, where the share prices fell back subsequent to their issue.

The FTSE Small Cap Index[6] has also performed poorly, although the reasons for this are not so easy to prove. It is believed to be related to the relative constriction of access to credit and the ongoing reduction of pension fund allocations to UK small capitalisation stocks.

At the micro-cap end of the market there are the RBS HG1000[7] and the FTSE Fledgling indices.[8] The latter includes most of the fully listed companies that are deemed too small in market capitalisation terms for the FTSE All-Share index. Both the RBS HG1000 and the FTSE Fledgling have performed better than the FTSE Small Cap index. This might have been expected since the HG1000 and the FTSE Fledgling are made up of

---

6   FTSE SmallCap: Companies outside the FTSE 350 Index, representing approx 2% of total market capitalisation

7   Covered in Chapter 7

8   FTSE Fledgling: Listed on the London Stock Exchange but too small to be listed on the FTSE All Share Index

much smaller businesses than the FTSE Small Cap. The smaller company effect has improved their performance.

The big fault line is seen in the differential performance between the FTSE Small Cap, which contains smaller businesses than the FTSE 250.[9] The FTSE 250 has outperformed the FTSE Small Cap by a very large percentage. **Clearly the benefit of access to debt has been a very favourable factor over the period of the debt boom and this has almost completely obscured the small company effect.**

The effect of the credit boom has held up the natural outperformance of smaller companies, as larger companies' easy access to debt enhanced their returns for a long period. So smaller companies might be expected to outperform in the coming years for two reasons:

- The usual smaller company effect reasserts itself as the credit boom ends;
- Companies that are relatively under-borrowed are likely to see a catch-up in their performance.

---

9   FTSE 250: Mid-sized companies listed on the London Stock Exchange, representing just under 15% of total market capitalisation

Bibliography

Introduction
Print:

Juster, N. *The Phantom Tollbooth*. 4th edition. London: HarperCollins, 2002.

Kay, J. *The Truth about Markets: Why Some Countries Are Rich and Others Are Poor*. London: Penguin, 2004.

Lanchester, J. *Whoops! Why Everybody Owes Everyone and No one Can Pay*. London: Penguin, 2010.

Chapter 1
Print:

Anastassova-Chirmiciu, L. *The Evolution of UK and London Employment Rates*. London: Greater London Authority, 2008.

Barnett-Hart, A.K. 'The Story Of The CDO Market Meltdown: An empirical analysis', 2009. Boston: Harvard University. www.hks.harvard.edu/m-rcbg/students/dunlop/2009-CDOmeltdown.pdf

Black, F. and M. Scholes 'The Pricing of Options and Corporate Liabilities'. *The Journal of Political Economy*. Chicago: University of Chicago Press. Vol. 81, No. 3. (May – June, 1973) (1973) pp. 637–654.

City of London Employment Report 1999–2009. London: City of London, 2009.

Crotty, J. 'Structural Causes of the global financial crisis: a critical assessment of the "new financial architecture"'. Cambridge: *Cambridge Journal of Economics*. Vol. 33 Issue 4. (2009) pp. 563–580.

Fama, E.F. and K.R French. 'The Capital Asset Pricing Model: Theory and Evidence'. *Journal of Economic Perspectives*. Pittsburgh: AEA Publications. Vol. 18, Number 3. (2004) pp. 25–46.

House of Commons. 'Banking Crisis: dealing with the failure of the UK Banks'. London: The Stationery Office. Treasury Select Committee, Seventh Report of Session 2008–09. (2009) p. 31.

Hunt, A. 'Investment Review – Life on Mars?' *Andrew Hunt Economics* 14th April 2010.

Merhling, P. *The New Lombard Street: How the Fed became the Dealer of Last Resort*. New Jersey: Princeton University Press, 2010.

Paxton, Angela. *The Food Miles Report: The dangers of long-distance food transport* SAFE Alliance, 1994.

'Rise of the machines: Algorithmic trading causes concern among investors and regulators', The Economist, 30th July 2009.

'The uses and abuses of mathematical models'. *The Economist*. 11th February 2011.

Online:

Bank for International Settlements: Semi-annual OTC statistics www.bis.
  org/statistics/derstats.htm

Berry, R.P 'Value at Risk: An overview of analytical *VaR*'. JP Morgan Analytics
  and Consulting, 2010. www.jpmorgan.com/tss/General/Risk_Management/
  1159360877242

Emergency loans from Bank of England to retail banks: http://uk.reuters.
  com/article/2009/11/25/uk-britain-banks-emergency   idUKTRE5AO1
  NI20091125?feedType=RSS&feedName=topNews

Employment Trends, Department of Planning and Transportation. City of
  London Employment Reports. City of London, 2011. www.cityoflondon.
  gov.uk/NR/rdonlyres/2480B451-CD2A-4BE6-8CA5-0D6568BB91DE/0/
  DP_PL_EmploymentTrends_2009BRESdata__1.pdf

Financial Stability Board. 'Potential financial stability issues arising from recent
  trends in Exchange-Traded Funds (ETFs)'. 2011. www.financialstabilityboard.
  org/publications/r_110412b.pdf

Mulholland, H., N. Watt and T. Macalister. 'UK debt interest bill will rise to
  £70bn without action, says David Cameron' *Guardian*. 7th June 2010
  www.guardian.co.uk/politics/2010/jun/07/cuts-change-british-way-of-
  life-david-cameron

IMF – Recession relative to 1930s: www.bloomberg.com/apps/news?pid=n
  ewsarchive&sid=aclg8HEIqKc4&refer=home

Lehmann's bankruptcy: http://www.guardian.co.uk/money/2007/sep/19/
  business

UK Debt Management Office: Gilt purchases in 2010: www.dmo.gov.uk/
  documentview.aspx?docname=publications/investorsguides/mb30 0610.
  pdf&page=investor_guide/Guide www.dmo.gov.uk/documentview.aspx?
  docname=publications/quarterly/oct-dec10.pdf&page=Quarterly_Review

World Bank – the scale of global economy: http://siteresources.worldbank.
  org/DATASTATISTICS/Resources/GDP.pdf

Chapter 2

Print:

Andrews, G. *The Slow Food Story: Politics and Pleasure*. Canada: McGill Queens
  University Press, 2008.

Blythman, J. *Bad Food Britain: How a Nation Ruined Its Appetite*. London:
  Fourth Estate, 2006.

Chi, K, J. MacGregor and R. King. *Fair Miles: Recharting the Fair Food Miles Map (Big Ideas in Development)*. London: International Institute for Environment and Development, 2009.

'Consumerism: Not by Cereal Alone'. *Time Magazine* (US edition). 17th August 1970.

'A Special report on Financial Risk'. *The Economist*. 11th February 2010.

Honoré, C. *In Praise of Slow: How a Worldwide Movement Is Challenging the Cult of Speed*. London: Orion Books, 2005.

Kay, J (2010) *Obliquity: Why Our Goals Are Best Achieved Indirectly*. London: Profile Books, 2010.

Marsh, D.B (ed). "The Bountiful Barbecue" in *The Good Housekeeping Cook Book*. New York: Rinehart and Company, 1955.

Nestle, M, Ludwig, D.S 'Front-of-Package Food Labels: Public Health or Propaganda?' Chicago: *Journal of the American Medical Association*. Vol. 303. (8) (2010) pp. 771–772.

Paxton, Angela. *The Food Miles Report: The Dangers of Long-distance Food Transport* SAFE Alliance, 1994.

Schlosser, E. *Fast Food Nation: What the All-American Meal Is Doing to the World*. London: Penguin Books, 2002.

Stern, J. and M. Stern. *Encyclopedia of Pop Culture*. New York: Harper Perennial, 1992.

Schumacher, E.F. *Small is Beautiful: A Study of Economics as if People Mattered*. London: Penguin Books, 1973.

'The Future of Securitisation'. UK: KPMG, 2011.

Online:

Achievements of Senator Choate: http://www.latimes.com/features/health/la-me-robert-choate17-2009may17,0,6130608.story

BBC The end of wartime rationing: http://news.bbc.co.uk/onthisday/hi/dates/stories/july/4/newsid_3818000/3818563.stm

'Consumerism: Not by Cereal Alone' *Time Magazine* (US edition). 17th August 1970: www.time.com/time/magazine/article/0,9171,909591-1,00.html

FDA guidance on food labels for consumers: http://www.fda.gov/ForConsumers/ConsumerUpdates/ucm094536.htm and http://www2.dupont.com/Heritage/en_US/1939_dupont/1939_indepth.html

Food Review Summary: http://www.nns.nih.gov/1969/executive_summary/exec_sum_2.htm

Food Trends from the 1950s: www.foodtimeline.org http://www.foodtimeline.org/fooddecades.html#tang

Global Food Industry: US Department of Agriculture Economic Research: www.ers.usda.gov/Briefing/GlobalFoodMarkets/Industry.htm

The Nixon food enquiry: http://nixon.archives.gov/forresearchers/find/textual/central/smof/whcofnh.php?print=yes

Chapter 3
Print:

Dimson, E, P. Marsh and M. Staunton. *Credit Suisse Global Investment Returns Yearbook*. Zurich: Credit Suisse AG. (2011) p. 12.

Dreman, D. *Contrarian Investment Strategies: Going against the Crowd*. New York: Simon & Schuster, 1998.

Graham, B. *The Intelligent Investor*. 4th edition. New York: Harper & Row, 1986.

LeBaron, D. (1974) 'A Psychological Profile of the Portfolio Manager: Have recent upheavals made the portfolio manager manic depressive, a game player, or too much the organization man?' Reprinted in *The Journal of Behavioural Finance and Investment Management*. December (2010) pp. 118–124.

Taleb, N.N. *Fooled by Randomness: The Hidden Role of Chance in Life and in the Markets*. London: Random House, 2008.

Taleb, N.N. *The Black Swan: The Impact of the Highly Improbable*. London: Random House, 2007.

Zeckhauser, R. *The Known, the Unknown, and the Unknowable in Financial Risk Management: Measurement and Theory Advancing Practice*. Edited by Diebold, Francis, Doherty, N. & Herring, H. New Jersey: Princeton University Press, 2010.

Zweig, J (2010) 'Fear'. *Behavioral Finance and Investment Management*. (December 2010) pp. 24–46

Chapter 4
Print:

Arnott, A, F. Li, and K. Sherrerd. 'Clairvoyant Value and the Value Effect'. (2009) *Journal of Portfolio Management*. 35.

Black, F. 'The Dividend Puzzle' *The Journal of Portfolio Management*. 4. (1976) pp. 634–639.

Davies, J.L, E.F Fama and K.R French. 'Characteristics, Covariances and Average Returns 1929–1997'. *Journal of Finance*. LV. 1. (2000)

Fama, E.F and K.R French. 'Value versus growth: The international evidence'. *Journal of Finance.* 53. 1975–1999. (1998)

Dimson, E, S. Nagel and G. Quigley. 'Capturing the Value Premium in the UK' *Financial Analysts Journal.* 59. 6. (2003) pp. 35–45.

Online:

Colombia Business School: http://www7.gsb.columbia.edu/valueinvesting/resources/articles

University of Chicago Library Bibliography for Eugene F. Fama: http://www.lib.uchicago.edu/e/busecon/busfac/Fama.html

Chapter 5

Print:

Arnott, A, F. Li, and K. Sherrerd.' Clairvoyant Value and the Value Effect'. *Journal of Portfolio Management.* 35. (2009) pp. 12–26.

Black, F. 'The Dividend Puzzle'. *The Journal of Portfolio Management.* 4. (1976) pp. 634–639.

Dimson E, Marsh, P (2011) RBS *HGSC Index Annual Report*

Dimson, E, P. Marsh and M. Staunton. *Credit Suisse Global Investment Returns Yearbook* . Zurich: Credit Suisse AG. (2011) p. 12 .

Dimson, E, S. Nagel and G. Quigley. 'Capturing the Value Premium in the UK' *Financial Analysts Journal.* 59. 6. (2003) pp. 35–45.

Miller, H.M, Modigliani, F. 'Dividend Policy, Growth and the Valuation of Shares'. *Journal of Business.* 34. (1961) pp. 411–433.

Online:

'Barclays cuts asset finance to SMEs'. *Leasing World.* 16th February 2011: http://www.leasingworld.co.uk/freepages/news-detail.php?ID=651

Blackwell, David. 'Desire for dividends outweighs capital growth' *Financial Times.* 18th May 2011: www.ft.com/cms/s/0/c48405fa-8167-11e0-9c83-00144feabdc0.html?ftcamp=rss#axzz1PdSByaan

Chapter 6

Print:

Arnott, A, F. Li, and K. Sherrerd. 'Clairvoyant Value and the Value Effect'. *Journal of Portfolio Management.* 35. (2009) pp. 12–26

Dimson, E, P. Marsh and M. Staunton. *Credit Suisse Global Investment Returns Yearbook* . Zurich: Credit Suisse AG. (2011) p. 12

Hunt, A. 'China: A Public Sector Boom' *Andrew Hunt Economics*. 3rd February 2011.

Lucas, R. 'Why doesn't Capital Flow from Rich to Poor Countries?' *American Economic Review*. 80. 2. (2005) pp. 92–96.

Kay, J. *The Truth about Markets: Why some nations are rich but most remain poor*. New York: Harper Paperbacks, 2003.

Merrill Lynch economist Ting Lu. 'Revisiting China's empty city of Ordos' *Wall Street Journal*. 12th May 2010.

Chapter 7

Print:

Ashkenas, R. *Simply Effective: How to Cut Through Complexity in Your Organization and Get Things Done*. Boston: Harvard Business School Press, 2009.

Ashkenas, R. cited in Cunha, M.P. 'Complexity, simplicity, simplexity'. Lisbon: University of Lisbon. Prepared for *Organisational Studies Workshop*, Cyprus 2008.

Davies, J.L, E.F Fama and K.R French. 'Characteristics, Covariances and Average Returns 1929–1997'. (2000). *Journal of Finance*. LV. 1.

Hunt, A. 'Investment Review – Life on Mars?' *Andrew Hunt Economics* 14th April 2010.

Patnaik, D. (2011) 'Why can't big companies solve big problems?'. Fast Company for Jump http://www.jumpassociates.com/why-cant-big-companies-solve-big-problems-2.html

Söderbom, M. and Y. Sato. 'Are larger firms more productive due to scale economies? A contrary evidence from Swedish Microdata'. University of Gothenburg (2011).

'The law of large numbers'. *Citibank Investment Research & Analysis*. 30th June 2008.

Zeckhauser, R. (2006) reprinted in *The Known, the Unknown, and the Unknowable in Financial Risk Management: Measurement and Theory Advancing Practice*. Edited by Diebold, F, N. Doherty and R. Herring. New Jersey: Princeton University Press, 2010. Examples cited include evolving medical technologies including neo-organ development

Online:

Patnaik, D. (2011) 'Why can't big companies solve big problems?' Fast Company for Jump http://www.jumpassociates.com/why-cant-big-companies-solve-big-problems-2.html

Stigler, G. (1963) cited in 'Smart Money'. *Wall Street Journal* 7th April 2011.

Chapter 8

Print:

Banz, R. 'The relationship between return and market value of common stocks'. *Journal of Financial Economics*. 9. (1981) pp. 13–18

Dimson, E, P. Marsh and M. Staunton. *Credit Suisse Global Investment Returns Yearbook*. Zurich: Credit Suisse AG. (2011) p. 12.

Fama E. and F. French. 'Value versus growth: The International Evidence 1975–1999'. *Journal of Finance*. 53. (6). (1998).

Graham, B. (1949) cited by D. Barker. (2010) 'Benjamin Graham's Investing Wisdom and Formula Timing Plans'. *The Market Oracle* 27th November 2010.

Malloy, C. *The Geography of Equity Analysis*. Boston: Harvard Business School NBER, 2003.

Miller, H.M. and F. Modigliani. 'Dividend Policy, Growth and the Valuation of Shares'. *Journal of Business*. (34). (1961) pp. 411–433.

Stigler, G. (1963) cited in 'Smart Money'. *Wall Street Journal*. 7th April 2011.

Online:

The Economist 'Dividends' end', 'Economics Focus'. 10th January 2002. http://www.economist.com/node/929911

Chapter 9

Print and online:

Turner, A. (2011) 'Reforming Finance: Are we being radical enough?' Clare Distinguished Lecture in Economics and Public Policy, Cambridge University, 19th February 2011. http://www.fsa.gov.uk/pages/Library/Communication/Speeches/2011/0218_at.shtml

Index